PASCAL

WITH

EXCELLENCE

Programming Proverbs

HENRY F. LEDGARD
WITH JOHN TAUER

Hayden Book Company

A DIVISION OF HAYDEN PUBLISHING COMPANY, INC.
HASBROUCK HEIGHTS, NEW JERSEY

Acquistions Editor: MICHAEL VIOLANO
Poduction Editor: ALBERTA BODDY
Text Design: JIM BERNARD
Cover Design: PAUL PERLOW
Composition: ART, COPY & PRINT COMPANY
Manufacturing: MALLOY LITHOGRAPHING, INC.

Sections of this book have been adapted from *Pascal with Style: Programming Proverbs*, by Henry F. Ledgard, Paul A. Nagin, and John F. Hueras, published in 1975 by Hayden Book Company.

Library of Congress Cataloging-in-Publication Data

Ledgard, Henry F.
    Pascal with excellence.

    Rev. ed. of: Programming proverbs. 1975.
    Bibliography
    Includes index.
    1. Pascal (Computer program language) I. Tauer, John. II. Legard, Henry F.,
Programming proverbs. III. Title.
QA76.73.P2L397   1986   005.13′3   86-277
ISBN 0-8104-6490-X

Printed in the United States of America

	1	2	3	4	5	6	7	8	9	
	86	87	88	89	90	91	92	93	94	YEAR

FOREWORD

By necessity, computer science, computer education, and computer practice are all embryonic human activities, for they have existed for only a single generation. From the beginning, programming has been a frustrating black art, with individual abilities ranging from the excellent to the ridiculous and often exhibiting very little in the way of systematic mental procedure. In a sense, the teaching of programming through mistakes and debugging can hardly be regarded as legitimate university-level course work. At the university level we teach such topics as the notion of an algorithm, concepts in programming languages, compiler design, operating systems, information storage and retrieval, artificial intelligence, and numerical computation; but in order to implement ideas in any of these functional activities, we need to write programs in a specific language.

Students and professionals alike tend to be overly optimistic about their ability to write programs or to make programs work according to preestablished design goals. However, we are beginning to see a breakthrough in programming as a mental process. This breakthrough is based more on considerations of style than on detail. It involves taking style seriously, not only in how programs look when they are completed, but in the very mental processes tha create them. In programming, it is not enough to be inventive and ingenious. One also needs to be disciplined and controlled in order not to become entangled in one's own complexities.

In any new area of human activity, it is difficult to foresee latent human capabilities. We have many examples of such capabilities: touch typing, speed writing, and 70-year-old grandmothers who drive down our highways at 70 miles per hour. Back in 1900, it was possible to foresee cars going 70 miles per hour, but the drivers were imagined as daredevils rather than as grandmothers. The moral is that in any new human activity one generation hardly scratches the surface of its capabilities. So it will be in programming as well.

The next generation of programmers will be much more competent than the first. They will have to be. Just as it was easier to get into college in the "good old days," it was also easier to get by as a programmer in the "good old days." For this new generation, a programmer will need to be capable of a level of precision and productivity never dreamed of before.

This new generation of programmers will need to acquire discipline and control, mainly by learning to write programs correctly from the start. The debugging process will take the new form of verifying that no errors are present, rather than the old form of finding and fixing errors over and over (otherwise known as "acquiring confidence by exhaustion"). Programming is a serious logical business that requires concentration and precision. In this discipline, concentration is highly related to confidence.

In simple illustration, consider a child who knows how to play a perfect game of tic-tac-toe but does not know that he knows. If you ask him to play for something important, like a candy bar, he will say to himself, "I hope I can win." And sometimes he will win, and sometimes not. The only reason he does not always win is that he drops his concentration. He does not realize this fact because he regards winning as a chance event. Consider how different the situation is when the child *knows* that he knows how to play a perfect game of tic-tac-toe. Now he does not say, "I hope I can win." He says instead, "I know I can win; it's up to me!" And he recognizes the necessity for concentration in order to ensure that he wins.

In programming, as in tic-tac-toe, it is characteristic that concentration goes hand in hand with justified confidence in one's own ability. It is not enough simply to know how to write programs correctly. The programmer must *know that he knows* how to write programs correctly, and then supply the concentration to match.

This book of proverbs is well suited to getting members of the next generation off to the right start. The elements of style discussed here can help provide the mental discipline to master programming complexity. In essence, the book can help a programmer make a large first step on the road to a new generation of programming.

HARLAN D. MILLS

Federal Systems Division, IBM
Gaithersburg, Maryland

PREFACE

🐦

Pascal with Excellence: Programming Proverbs was originally motivated by a small book called *The Elements of Style*, written by William Strunk, Jr., and revised by E.B. White. Originally conceived in 1918, Strunk's book stresses the need for rigor, conciseness, and clarity in the writing of English prose. In like manner, *Pascal with Excellence* is intended for Pascal programmers who want to write carefully constructed, readable programs.

Many programmers have told of programming experiences in which a simple set of guidelines could have averted disaster. Although a burned hand may teach a good lesson, the introduction of well-advised guidelines is an easier and less painful way to achieve good programming. To be sure, guidelines restrict the programmer. However, the hope is to enable the programmer to focus creativity on the deeper issues in programming rather than on problems that obscure the issues.

Several characteristics other than academic ones have been deliberately sought in this book. First, there has been an attempt to be lighthearted. The intention is to encourage a zest for learning that we all need in order to do our more rewarding work. Second, there has been an attempt to be specific. Progress is made when we speak plainly and give examples of what we say.

The programming examples are given in Pascal, but the points of the examples should be clear even without a detailed knowledge of the Pascal language. The programs given here conform to the definition of Pascal as presented in Jensen and Wirth (1985) and conform to the standard definition of Pascal (see Pascal, 1983). The bibliography at the end of the book lists all references.

This book is designed as a guide to better programming, not as an introduction to the details of Pascal or a similar higher-level language. It should be of value to all programmers who have some familiarity with Pascal. As such, it may be used as a supplement in courses where Pascal programming is a major concern, or as an informal guide to those who have an interest in improving software quality. However, I strongly believe that the ideas presented should go hand in hand with learning the Pascal language itself.

The reader who dismisses the overall objective of this book with the comment "I've got to learn all about Pascal first" may be surprised to find that the study of good programming practices in conjunction with the basics of the language may reap quick and longstanding rewards.

Pascal with Excellence is organized in three major parts. After the opening statement of the Introduction, Part I features a collection of simple rules, called *proverbs*. The proverbs summarize in terse form the major ideas of this book. Each proverb is explained and applied. There are a few references to later chapters where various ideas are more fully explored.

Part II, on program standards, discusses the programming conventions used in this book. These rules have been strictly followed here, and I believe that their adoption is one key factor in achieving quality programs. The section also elaborates on several important and sometimes controversial ideas discussed in Part I on programming proverbs.

Part III captures the point of the entire text with an example of a strict top-down approach to a programming problem. The approach is oriented toward the easy writing of complete, correct, readable programs. The approach hinges on developing the overall logical structure of the program first. Moreover, the programming proverbs are brought into action during the program's development. This section concludes with a full-scale program, given in Appendix B. The program is intended as a model of good programming.

This work is based on several predecessors, the so-called "Programming Proverbs" series, which includes *Programming Proverbs, Programming Proverbs for Fortran Programmers, Cobol with Style, Basic with Style, Fortran with Style,* and, notably, *Pascal with Style.*

Paul Nagin and Jon Hueras, co-authors of *Pascal with Style,* helped write and improve the programs in this earlier work. They are both gentlemen of high professional standard and were a pleasure to work with.

William Fastie, Joseph Davison, and Leslie Chaikin were the spirited sources of many ideas taken from the early members of this series. Louis Chmura, Andrew Singer, Michael Marcotty, and William Cave strongly influenced the ideas presented here. Louis Chmura, co-author of *Cobol with Style*, helped set the original proverbs on an even higher level of quality. Andrew Singer was the source of a stimulating critique of the whole area of programming. Michael Marcotty set an example of clear programming style. William Cave provided provocative discussions on the writing of large programming systems for day-to-day use. I am truly grateful to all.

The motivation for writing this book is largely the result of my experience in teaching professional programmers at Philips Electronics in Europe. These courses were under the brilliant direction of Allen Macro, assisted by John Buxton. The participants in the courses, together with my colleague Nat Macon, deepened by commitment to excellence.

Pascal with Excellence is basically my personal statement about programming. Above all else, I firmly believe that the study of guidelines for good programming can be of great value to all programmers and that there are principles that transcend the techniques of any individual practitioner.

TO THE READER

In a profession where change is the order of the day, program-mers tend to be thrown off the foundations on which the profes-sion was built. Two mutually self-serving forces, I think, are at work here. First, we rush for solutions often before we examine the problem in depth. Sometimes we succeed. But we pay a price. The price is software that is far from excellent, both in its user interface and its underlying quality.

Second, I think we take ourselves too seriously. The way we write user manuals leaps to mind as indicative of an undue concern for technical compliance with no regard for the reader. We are, indeed, involved with frontiers. But we tend to lose touch with people as we rush to the terminal.

This book is a two-fold response to these observations. First, the programming proverbs represent years of thinking about some basic issues. I have worked with programmers for many years. In almost every case, I have been disappointed and said little, knowing that it is hard to change any habit. The top-down approach, for instance, is nothing new but is simply an orderly method of returning to the basics of programming.

And second, this work is lighthearted in many ways. The ap-proach is not directed away from the technical issues but toward conveying key ideas with good spirit. The purpose is to teach the fledgling and remind the veteran that certain princi-ples need to be reviewed now and again. My hope is to convey a sense of what it means to produce quality work.

CONTENTS

P A R T
ONE

PROGRAMMING PROVERBS

INTRODUCTION

❦

"I HAVE SEEN THE FUTURE, AND IT WORKS."

Lincoln Steffens

Whenever anyone discusses the "state of the art" in any discipline or profession, the purpose is to make a statement of what "is" to what "can be" or what "ought to be." This was an inherent objective of the earlier editions of the Programming Proverb series. Now, many years later, it is somewhat disheartening for me to report that what "was" still "is."

Seldom are the results of a programming development project concluded with a proud exclamation: "It worked right the first time!" That programs seldom work right the first time is not the only indication of the state of the art. Sometimes programs work only part of the time; some never work at all. Of the ones that do, their utility is lost in the arduous and often painful effort to maintain them. Writing high-quality programs is possible, but unusual. I ask the question: why is the product program so poor so often; that is, why don't programmers succeed more often? The reasons are simple. First, programming is difficult, especially as programmers must keep pace with an expanding and demanding technology. Ours is a profession that is never static, even from one project to the next.

Second, there are very few principles for developing and writing good programs. We tend to think that the principles of programming lie in the perfection and execution of the algorithm itself and, once we have learned the programming language, all that needs to be known is understood. The result is that programmers develop procedures to work around the difficulties of programming—procedures that are often developed in the heat of development—but they have few *principles* to rely on for real success.

The concern of the computer industry about the quality of software has persisted for many years. Surely the time has come for programmers to write programs that work correctly the first time—or at least the tenth or twentieth time—programs that do the job even when the original problem was poorly conceived; programs that are easy to read, understand, and maintain.

Some may think attempts to correct such practices are unrealistic, especially considering their past experiences of constant revision, debugging, and difficulties in deciphering code. There are, however, well-founded principles that can be utilized to achieve these goals. Some of these principles I shall present are obvious, even to novice programmers. Others—even experienced programmers—might debate this. However, before any principle is rejected, it must be remembered that a program is not only a set of descriptions and instructions for a computer, but *a set of descriptions and instructions that must be understood by human beings*. For you, the programmer, first of all, and for all others who will read your program in the process from development to maintenance.

It is well-known that the cost of program development and maintenance is high and growing higher. In fact, I have heard it said that the cost of program maintenance on some poorly constructed systems is a hundred times greater than the cost of initial development and testing. To attack these costs, methodology and clarity must be early programming concerns.

Although the development of effective algorithms and data structures is an important activity that is closely related to general programming techniques, this is not the focus here. The issue here is how to help the programmer write clear programs of impeccable quality. With this in mind, the programming proverbs are the motivation for this book.

As with most maxims or proverbs, the rules are not absolute—but neither are they arbitrary. Each proverb is a reservoir of thought and experience. At first glance, some of them may seem trivial or too time-consuming to follow. But they were written to be succinct and useful, much (I hope) like Ben Franklin's simple maxims that he collected as a guide to every-day living in his *Poor Richard's Almanac*. Like old saws, the proverbs overlook much important detail in favor of easily remembered phrases. Indeed, there are some cases where programs should not conform to standard rules; that is, there are exceptions to every proverb. Nevertheless, experience will show that these exceptions are rare and that a programmer should not violate these rules without serious reasons to do so.

A list of the proverbs is given in Figure 1. The proverbs are further related to a relative timing process of development (DEV), documentation (DOC), coding (CODE), testing (TEST), debugging (DEBUG), and maintenance and modification (M&M). This figure suggests their relative impact on programming.

Figure 1   *Matrix summary of THE PROGRAMMING PROVERBS*

	DEV	DOC	CODE	TEST	DEBUG	M&M
Chapter 1. *A Good Start Is Half the Race*						
1 Don't Panic	★★					
2 Question the Problem	★★	★				
3 Define the Problem	★	★★	★			★
4 Document First	★	★★★	★			★
5 Think First, Code Later			★★★	★		★
6 Proceed Top-Down			★	★	★	★★★
7 Beware of Other Approaches			★★		★	★
Chapter 2. *Structure Is Logic*						
8 Code It for the Other Guy			★		★★	★★★
9 Don't Nest					★	★
10 Black-Box Your Subroutines				★★	★★★	★★★
11 Don't Goto			★		★	★

		DEV	DOC	CODE	TEST	DEBUG	M&M
Chapter 3. *Coding the Program*							
12	All Words Mean Something			★ ★		★	★ ★
13	Spaces Have Meaning, Too			★		★	★ ★
14	Comment for Content				★		★
15	Make Constants Constant			★ ★			★ ★
16	Name All Types			★		★	★
17	Get the Syntax Correct Now			★ ★			
18	Remember Your Reader						★ ★ ★
19	Your Output Is Not Only for You		★		★ ★		
20	Review, Review, Review				★	★	★
21	Careful Programmers Don't Have Accidents				★	★	
Chapter 4. *And of Course . . .*							
22	Have Someone Else Read the Work	★ ★	★ ★	★ ★	★ ★	★ ★	★ ★ ★
23	What Have You Read Lately?	★ ★	★ ★				
24	Don't Be Afraid to Start Over				★ ★	★ ★	
	Total	**10**	**11**	**20**	**13**	**18**	**30**

Note: The stars indicate my subjective evaluation of the relative values of the processes indicated.

The relative importance of one proverb over another depends quite markedly on the problem at hand. By assigning a relative value to each proverb based on observation and experience (as in Figure 1), the graph in Figure 2 indicates the overall effect of the proverbs during program development.

In closing this introduction, note that the word "proverb" is used, rather than the more accurate word "maxim." Proverbs and maxims both refer to pithy sayings derived from practical experience. Proverbs are usually well known, whereas maxims are not. Admittedly, the programming proverbs are not in themselves popular sayings; however, the title was chosen with an idea to the future. I hope these proverbs will assist programmers in joining Lincoln Steffens in seeing the future with the confidence that it will work.

Figure 2   ***Overall impact of the proverbs***

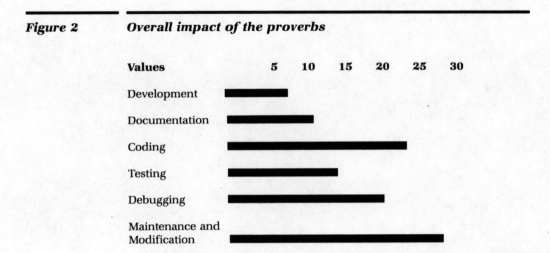

1 *A GOOD START IS HALF THE RACE*

"FIRST ESTABLISH THE MAIN PRINCIPLES, AND THE SMALL DETAILS CANNOT GET AWAY."

Mencius
Cofounder of Confucianism

Proverb 1   *DON'T PANIC*   *"The world belongs to the enthusiast who keeps cool."*
WILLIAM MCFEE   *Casuals of the Sea, Book I*

Most programming projects are the result of a need for a new piece of software to solve a new problem or the need to modify and improve a functioning piece of software. There should be a thoughtful prelude to the project, but at the moment of inception, panic begins to reign when reason is needed most. The causes are as varied as the personalities that attend them. More often than not, a programmer is loaded down with other work of equal importance. Instructors or management may put pressure on you by setting an unrealistic schedule. You may need to finish before the semester ends, or there may be a bonus for completing by some deadline. There is a tendency for the enthusiastic programmer to "get on with the job," i.e., code, code, code. Overlooking this first programming proverb results in a tendency to obtain speedy results—this is counter to all good programming practices.

Good sense must prevail. The same thoughtful approach that defined the project must be carried into the initial phases of the project before coding is begun. To rush in panic to the terminal will surely result in a situation that is all too common

9

today, where existing code must constantly be reworked as new code shows oversights, where bugs hide all over the finished code, and maintenance takes longer than expected.

This advice applies to programmers and project managers alike: if you find yourself plowing ahead with a new programming assignment, don't panic.

1. *Stop.*

2. *Calm down.*

3. *Return to methodical programming techniques that work.*

Time is your ally. Sometimes, if the enthusiast takes the afternoon off, he or she will discover what can be done in the cool of the evening.

Proverb 2   *Question the Problem*

Programmers must recognize the difference between solving a puzzle and solving a programming problem. There is only one solution to a puzzle, but a problem often comes begging its own definition. A puzzle may be simply rearranging pieces on a card table until the picture stands before us; it may be finding the elusive definition that fills in the last square of a crossword. But a programming problem asks the examiner to question the premise of the problem itself.

More often than not, programmers are handed a problem to be solved—not a puzzle to be solved. Someone else invents the problem. Most likely, there will be a written description of the problem. The first impulse is to take the problem as stated. Watch out! This is the difference between a puzzle and a problem.

There are two almost universal difficulties with the statement of a problem or, as it is often referred to, the "specification" of a problem:

1. *The problem is not fully specified.*
   There may be gaping omissions and inconsistencies.

2. *The problem itself can be better defined.*

This proverb addresses the second point.

Consider the small problem definition of Figure 3a. It is set in type, looks unnegotiable, and may even seem reasonable. Stop. Why do the inputs need to be in columns? As stated,

```
20000  8.00   22-1
```

is a fine input, but

```
20000 8.00 22 -1
```

is not. Thus, input is tedious and error prone. And why –1, not a "?" or –9? How will the computer read –1 when (say, for the percentage) a fixed-point real number is requested? And who will remember the order of inputs? How will the user know what to input? For a small problem, this is a fast start to trouble.

Figure 3b gives a more inspired problem definition. The difference may not seem great, but it is certainly better for the human user, and probably easier to implement as well.

Figure 3.   *Proposed definitions of a mortgage problem*

(a) Poor Problem Definition

We wish to devise a program to help potential homeowners assess the finances of mortgaging a home. There are four basic factors to be considered: the principal, the interest rate, the number of years for the mortgage, and the monthly payment. The program must input values for any three of the above quantities, output the fourth quantity, and also output a table indicating how the amount of the first monthly payment of each year is divided between principal and interest.

The input to this program is a line containing three of the above four factors:

Columns	Quantity
1-5	Principal
8-12	Interest Rate
15-16	Number of years
17-23	Monthly payments

The principal and number of years are given as integers, the interest rate and monthly payments are given as fixed-point real numbers. The missing quantity is given as –1.

The output is to be a line indicating the value of the missing quantity, and a table giving, for the first monthly payment of each year, the amount contributed to decreasing the principal and the amount paid as interest.

(b) Better Problem Definition

We wish to devise a program to help potential homeowners assess the finances of mortgaging a home. There are four basic factors to be considered: the principal, the interest rate, the number of years for the mortgage, and the monthly payment. The program must obtain values for any three of the above quantities, output the fourth quantity, and also output a table indicating how the amount of the first monthly payment of each year is divided between principal and interest.

The program will prompt the user for the following four figures:

Quantity	Prompt
Principal	Enter Principal (in whole dollars):
Number of years	Enter Loan Period (in whole years):
Interest rate	Enter Interest Rate (to two decimal places):
Monthly payment	Enter Monthly Payment (to two decimal places):

The principal and number of years are given as integers, the interest rate and monthly payments are given as fixed-point real numbers. The missing quantity is given as zero.

The output is to be a line indicating the value of the missing quantity, and a table giving, for the first monthly payment of each year, the amount contributed to decreasing the principal and the amount paid as interest.

The miniature example above is not the odd case. Specifications written for programs will astound you! For instance:

1. *Far too many features*

2. *Unreadable prose*

3. *Confusing inputs or outputs*

4. *Baroque syntax for user notations*

5. *Overly complex solutions*

6. *Lack of thought to new versions*

7. *Strange punctuations for user notations*

8. *Impossible scheduling requirements*

9. *Cryptic messages*

10. *Etc., etc., etc.*

You cannot be discouraged. Your task is simply to question the problem that was given to you—it is not a puzzle, it is a problem . . . it comes with the territory. I have seen all these "problems with problems." Don't let them happen to you.

You should be reminded of John Stuart Mill's classic remark more than a hundred years ago:

"To question all things;—never to turn away from any difficulty; to accept no doctrine either from ourselves or from other people without a rigid scrutiny . . . these are the lessons we learn . . . ."

Questioning a problem in programming is, indeed, the lesson you must learn.

Proverb 3   **DEFINE THE PROBLEM**

"Nothing is difficult to a man who has persistence."
CHINESE PROVERB

Once satisfied with the rough specifications of a problem, you must tackle the task of defining the problem completely. This and the previous proverb are, perhaps, one: as you question the problem, the definition of the problem will become clear to you. Good problem definitions are vital to the construction of good programs. An incomplete or ill-formed definition implies that the problem is not fully understood. Missing information, ignorance of special cases, and an abundance of extraneous information in a definition are good signs of poor programs or, at best, of programs that will be a surprise for the ultimate user. Any program that processes large amounts of data is bound to encounter some simple unnoticed condition, resulting in the all too common program crash.

We have often heard the claim that it is quite permissible to start with an imperfect problem definition, for during later program development a good programmer will readily pick up any critical points missed in the initial definition. This is a dangerous premise as it is counter to all the principles of professional programming. Starting with solid, complete program definition is laborious and requires persistence. But it is often half the solution to the entire problem. Moreover, good definitions will serve as the basis for good program documentation, and make programming itself easier.

There are many reasons why good problem definitions are rare. First, there is no well-accepted idea of what comprises a good definition. Different programmers, instructors, and managers usually employ different definition techniques. For example, some project managers require only program narratives, decision tables, or system flowcharts. Another common practice is to have an experienced systems analyst draw up several system flowcharts, some narrative descriptions, and some detailed descriptions of some inputs and outputs. Of course, the quality and completeness of these definitions will vary according to the style of the individual analyst.

Second, as we noted in the first proverb, there is an almost irresistible temptation to skirt over the issue of definition in order to "get on with the job." This temptation is especially acute when the given problem is similar to previously solved problems or when there is strong external pressure to produce some quick, visible results (that is, programs). Furthermore, even if programmers could avoid the rush to get on with the job, management and the "customer" often make it difficult to invest the time and money in a good problem definition. The results of good definitions often appear to be wasted, since working code is usually delayed, especially when a programmer works hard to ensure that no problem situations go unnoticed.

Third, good problem definitions involve plain hard work. There is an intense amount of persistence and discipline required to get any definition straight.

As an example, consider the earlier definition of Figure 3b, which defined a program to aid a prospective homeowner in determining the financial arrangements of a mortgage loan. The definition might appear adequate, but on closer analysis many points need to be resolved:

1. *How are the principal, number of years, interest rate, and monthly payments related? Is there a formula?*

2. *Where are the prompts?*

3. *Are the ranges for each value adequate?*

4. *What input errors can arise?*

5. *Why can't we see a sample of the input/output?*

6. *What is the format of the table?*

7. *Does the table have headings?*

8. *Are numbers like "20,000" allowed?*

These decisions will have to be made eventually. Now is the time. The definition in Figure 4 resolves each of the above issues. Although longer, it is more precise than that of Figure 3b.

One important point of Figure 4 is the inclusion of a sample of the input and output. Often a simple dialogue or printout can be of great value to a program in giving a quick synopsis of the problem. In addition, a sample can prevent surprises in cases where the program turns out to be quite different from the expectations of the person defining the program. If a programmer is not given a sample of the input-output, he or she should try to provide it before programming. It is a pity that samples are so rarely done, as though we in our own trade are hiding from the real problems we are committed to solve.

Figure 4.   ***Clarified definition of a mortgage problem***

(1) Problem Outline   We wish to devise a program to help potential homeowners assess the finances of mortgaging a home. There are four basic quantities to be considered:

P   The principal amount of the mortgage
I   The yearly interest rate for the mortgage
N   The number of years for the duration of the mortgage
M   The constant monthly payment required to pay back the principal P over N years at the interest rate I.

These quantities are related by the equation:

$$M = \frac{P * i * (1 + i)^n}{(i + i)^n - 1}$$

where

> I = 1/12 = monthly interest rate
> N = 12*N = number of monthly periods in N years

Briefly, the program is to input any three of the above quantities, compute and print the fourth quantity, and also print a table specifying how the first monthly payment of each year is divided between interest and principal.

(2) Input   The program will prompt the user for the values of P, N, I, and M. These have the general form

> P: ddddd
> N: dd
> I: dd.dd
> M: ddd.dd

where the d's represent decimal digits such that

> P = the principal in dollars
> N = the number of years in integer form
> I   = the percentage interest rate computed to two
>   decimal places
> M = the monthly payment in dollars and cents

The value of P, I, N, or M to be computed is given as zero. Additional or fewer digits (than those shown above) are allowed. However, each whole number must have at least one digit, and each decimal point number must have at least one digit on each side of the decimal point. Except to the right of a decimal point, leading zeros may be replaced by blanks.

(3) Output   The output from the program is to consist of two parts: (a) The value to be computed, using one of the formats:

```
PRINCIPAL           = $dddddd
NUMBER OF YEARS     = dd
INTEREST RATE       = dd.dd
MONTHLY PAYMENT     = $dddd.dd
```

and (b) A table giving for the first monthly payment of each year the amount paid to principal and the amount paid to interest. The headings and formats for the table values are as follows:

```
YEAR   AMT TO PRINCIPAL   AMT TO INTEREST
 dd         $ddd.dd            $ddd.dd
```

Except to the right of a decimal point, leading zeros for any value are to be replaced by blanks.

(4) Exceptional Conditions   If any of the input values are not in the prescribed format, the user is to be prompted for the value again. If any output value is not in the range indicated, the program is to print an appropriate message to the user.

(5) Sample Input   The principal, number of years, interest rate, and monthly payment of a mortgage are required below. Enter three values, and enter 0 for the value to be computed.

Enter principal (in whole dollars): <u>20000</u>
Enter loan period (in whole years): <u>25</u>
Enter interest rate (to two decimal places): <u>8.0%</u>
**Value not recognized. Try again: <u>8.00</u>
Enter monthly payment (to two decimal places): <u>0</u>

(6) Sample Output for Above Input

```
MONTHLY PAYMENT = $154.36

YEAR   AMT TO PRINCIPAL   AMT TO INTEREST
  1         21.03             133.33
  2         22.77             131.59
  .
  .
  .
 25        142.53              11.83
```

In Chapter 5, we will discuss several ideas for producing good problem definitions in conjunction with a complete example. However, there are a few points about good definitions that deserve to be mentioned here. First, in attempting to supply a complete problem definition, the programmer probably cannot err by devoting extra time and thought. While perfect definitions are probably unattainable, with good technique and discipline, you will end up "close" to one. Remember that all languages have rigid rules for the execution of programs, and programmers must be specific to the last detail. If something is left unspecified in the original definition, the programmer will eventually have to face the consequences. At best, the changes that must be made are frustrating and distracting.

Once you believe that a definition is complete, put it aside for a while. Pick it up later, reread and rethink it—this is genuine persistence. Better still, have someone else read it (see Proverb 22). The problem definitions thought to be "complete" may reveal flaws by the light of a new day or the cool of another evening. You will find that most of these proverbs apply simultaneously to any problem you have. As a final word, make sure that you have a complete written description of the problem before you do anything else.

Proverb 4   *Document First*

What can be said in one short proverb about a subject that has been cussed and discussed for years? Many have tried to define and analyze program documentation, to motivate programmers to understand that the central purpose of documentation is to provide effective communication of factual information among people. The most important aspect of documentation is not just to do it early, but to do it first. You will be in close touch with your user's or instructor's requirements so that your understanding of the required program will be greatly enhanced.

What is "documentation" in the sense that we define it here? It could be:

1. *In a class exercise, a summary of program design.*

2. *In a class project, a manual or write-up of how to use the program.*

3. *In a commercial project, a reference manual or user's guide.*

4. *In a contracted piece of software, an installation manual or user's guide.*

Very often, it comes down to:

1. *The comments at the beginning of a program.*

2. *The user manual.*

Now, very few programmers do these things before coding. Why?

Because documentation takes effort. And because, more often than not, it appears to be a drudgery. It is easy to hide from hard work, to consider it premature if not impossible. Rubbish.

> "There is quite a difference between 'I can't do it' and 'I won't do it.' Usually it is the latter."
>
> Mencius

Doing the documentation first is a powerful design tool. It ferrets out the nebulous ideas and clarifies them in the mind of the programmer. The user will never be able to read your thoughts or sketchy notes as you begin a project, but he will surely read your preliminary user manual. If you do the documentation first, you will put the user first. In so doing, you will expose the details of the program for yourself. Oddly enough, doing the documentation first is more rewarding because, as the project proceeds, delaying documentation compounds the difficulty and it becomes a chore.

On major programming projects, the better ones, good documentation is identified by several characteristics:

1. *Readability is the major goal. Documentation is meant to be read by other human beings. With proper documentation, the reader does not have to stare at a shelf of material with no idea of where to begin.*

2. *Documentation is considered important. The what, when, and how of good documentation are recorded somewhere (i.e., standardized), and help is available to understand the standards.*

3. *The required documentation is planned from the beginning. Some documents are written long before others and serve as guides for the later ones.*

4. *Documentation is part of the daily programming process. Finger paralyzing treatises on long-forgotten topics are not needed. The documentation system drives the programming process!*

5. *There is no pressure to skimp. Someone asks for needed documentation, someone else reads it, and the end reward is the production of high-quality documentation.*

In all honesty, documentation is rarely as good as all this. It is possible to be involved in a programming project with a less than perfect documentation system. The point is that, in this event, it is incumbent upon you to develop your own ideas and procedures early.

We all should be able to recognize good documentation. The only thing left to do is to begin providing it. While you may not achieve good documentation right away, any step in that direction is to be preferred to the confusion that will result if you delay documentation later in the project. Try it once. You will see the point.

Proverb 5	*THINK FIRST,* *CODE LATER*	*"Man is obviously made to think."* PASCAL

There is as much literature on the mechanics of the golf swing as there is on the mechanics of programming. Without exception, professional golfers have mastered the mechanics of the golf swing. But there is more. In a recent televised tournament, one such professional golfer was leading by two strokes going into the final hole. He placed his tee shot into a fairway bunker, tried to reach the green and hit a greenside bunker, bladed the next shot into a bunker on the other side of the green, pitched onto the green, two-putted for a six that tied the tournament, and then lost it on the first play-off hole. The television commentator asked in effect: "Why didn't he think? All he had to do was lay up out of the first bunker, pitch it on the green and two-putt for a five. He just didn't think!"

In much the same way, the mechanics of programming, relative to thinking about the problems of programming, can be mastered without undue difficulty. This proverb is intimately connected with the previous proverbs; the difference is that once the mechanical procedures of problem definition and documentation are finished, the essential task is to start thinking about the solution as soon as possible.

The proverb is literal: Think first means think—do not code! Start thinking while the problem is fresh in your mind and the deadline is as far away as it will ever be. Consider at least two different ways to solve the problem. Examine the approaches to discover possible trouble spots or areas where the solution appears difficult. Our professional golfer should have thought: the only way I can lose this tournament is to hit the ball into that greenside bunker. You should think that the only way this program will crash is if there is a faulty algorithm.

Code later means giving yourself time to weed out the difficult parts and polishing the algorithm before trying to formalize it in actual code. It is easier to clarify thoughts now than to discard poor programs later.

This proverb is most often violated by a "linear" approach to programming. This simply means that a programmer receives a problem and immediately starts preparing the code to solve it. Tempting as this approach may be, avoid it for it is full of hidden costs and dangers. Without thinking first, you may be coding for an ill-conceived program or—the ultimate foolishness—writing a program that you will have to throw away later.

In conclusion, remember Murphy's second law of programming: "it always takes longer to write a program than you think." A corollary might be: the sooner you start coding the program instead of thinking about it, the longer it will take to finish it.

| Proverb 6 | *PROCEED TOP-DOWN* | *"The last thing one settles in writing a book is what one puts in first."* PASCAL |

A major objective of this book is to advocate the "top-down" approach to programming problems. The top-down approach is itself subject to several interpretations, but many of these overlook important issues. Top-down programming is discussed at length in Chapter 7; however, following these rules of the top-down approach is the essence of this proverb:

1. *Design the top levels first.*

2. *Use language-independent forms initially.*

3. *Postpone details to lower levels.*

4. *Formalize each level.*

5. *Verify each level.*

6. *Make successive refinements.*

Consider the example in Figure 5. Here is the first pass at the top level for the programming problem of Chapter 7. Examining the definition of the problem, the programmer writes an informal program, P1 (first pass)in pseudo-code. After a more detailed look at the problem definition and considering the overall algorithm, the programmer develops P1 into a more refined version, P2 (second pass). The main program ultimately emerges and can be verified by testing. The code to produce the modules referenced in the final pass at the program must be developed in P2 and further refined in successive levels.

Top-down programming has two distinct advantages. First, a programmer is freed from the confines of a particular language and can deal with the more natural data structure of the program. Second, top-down programming leads to a modular approach that allows the programmer to write statements relevant to that program structure. The details can be developed later in separate modules. The main goal of top-down programming is to aid the programmer in writing well-structured, modular programs.

Figure 5.   ***Initial stages of program development***

P1 (First pass)

```
initialize program variables
welcome players

repeat
    get a proposed move
    if move is legal
        then process the move
    if the game is not over
        then change players
        else exit
until game over

end the game and stop
```

P2 (Second pass)

```
initialize (PLAYER, BOARD)
write (INTRODUCTORY_MESSAGES)

repeat
    get (MOVE) from PLAYER

    if LEGAL_MOVE (PLAYER, BOARD, MOVE) then
        UPDATE_BOARD (PLAYER, BOARD, MOVE)

        if LEGAL_JUMP (PLAYER, BOARD, MOVE)
        and JUMP_CAN_BE_CONTINUED (PLAYER, BOARD, MOVE) then
            CONTINUE_THE_JUMP (PLAYER, BOARD, MOVE)

        if NO_KING (BOARD, PLAYER)
        and MOVES_LEFT (BOARD, OPPONENT) then
            swap PLAYERS
            prompt OPPONENT for NEXT MOVE
        else
            write (WINNING_MSG) for PLAYER
            write (LOSING_MSG) for OPPONENT
            GAME_OVER is true
    else
        write (ILLEGAL_MOVE_MSG) for PLAYER
until GAME_OVER
```

The substance of this proverb will be amplified in Chapter 5. For now, Pascal's observation means this for the top-down approach: One does not write the first lines of the program first. One designs and writes the main control routine, the "top" level, first.

Proverb 7 | ### *BEWARE OF OTHER APPROACHES* | *"Beware of false prophets, which come to you in sheep's clothing, but inwardly are ravening wolves."*
MATTHEW VII: 12

---

1. *Bottom-up approach.*

2. *Inside-out approach.*

3. *Linear approach.*

4. *Typical systems analyst approach.*

5. *Imitation approach.*

Bottom-up Approach

In the "bottom-up" approach, the programmer writes the lower modules first and the upper levels later. This bottom-up approach is an inversion of the top-down approach. Its weakness lies in enticing the programmer to make specific decisions about the program before the overall problem and algorithm are understood.

Inside-out Approach

There are four other approaches to programming between the bottom-up and top-down. The "inside-out" or "forest" approach means, simply, starting in the middle of the program and working down and up at the same time. As such a method is convenient, it is therefore popular and needs closer examination. Roughly speaking, if we followed this approach, we would proceed as follows:

1. *General idea. First we decide on the general idea for programming the problem.*

2. *A rough sketch of the program. Next we write any sections of the program that we deem to be "important," assuming initialization in some form. In some sections we would write portions of the actual code.*

3. *Coding the first version. After Step 2, we write specific code for the entire program. After one module has been coded, we debug it, and immediately prepare a description of what it does.*

4. *Rethinking and revising. As a result of Step 3, we should be close to a working program, but it may be possible to improve it. So we continue by making several improvements until we obtain a complete working program.*

It is fair to say that many programmers work inside-out. Usually, they don't start very close to the top or the bottom of the program. Instead, they begin in the middle and work outward until a program finally emerges. This approach is obviously weak because as programs undergo patches and changes, there is no clear, logical structure for a programmer to follow.

Linear Approach

The third method is the "linear" approach that we introduced in Proverb 5. Here, one starts writing code as it will appear when executed: first line first, second line second, and so forth. This results in making specific detailed decisions with little assurance that they are appropriate to the problem at hand. Poor as this technique may appear to be, there is a strong temptation to employ it, especially on "easy" programs. But be particularly wary of this temptation: there is no such thing as an "easy" program.

Systems Analyst Approach

The fourth technique is the "systems analyst" approach. When used wisely, it can be an effective technique, and admittedly it has been successfully used for many large programs. We shall briefly compare it with the top-down approach, the technique advocated in this book.

The systems analyst often starts on a large programming problem by dividing up the task on the basis of the flow of control he sees in the overall program. The program is broken into a number of modules, which are then farmed out to the programmers. After these have been completed, the analyst will firm up the interfaces and try to make things work right. The lower-level modules receive special attention since their function and data handling are used often.

With the top-down approach, on the other hand, the flow of control is subservient to the logical structure. There does not have to be an identifiable flow of control that is easy to flowchart. The flow of control is rather like traversing a tree. It starts at the top level, goes down one or more levels, comes back, goes on to another level, and so forth. The top-down approach thus has little need for flowcharting.

Imitation Approach

A final method is what I call the "imitation" approach, a method superficially resembling the top-down approach. This approach is discussed in detail because many programmers think that the top-down approach is really the way they have always programmed. The imitation approach is described as follows:

1. *Thinking about the program. Having been given a programming assignment, take the time to examine the problem thoroughly before starting to program. Think about the details of the program for a while, and then decide on a general approach.*

2. *Deciding on submodules. After having thought about the problem in detail, decide on what sections will be sufficiently important to merit being made into submodules.*

3. *Data representation. After compiling a list of the submodules, decide on a data representation that will enable them to be efficient, unless the representation is already specified.*

4. *Coding of submodules. At this point, write each submodule. After each is completed, write down what it ex-*

pects as input, what it returns as output, and what it does. The submodules should be written in a hierarchical manner: the most primitive first, calling routines second, and so forth. Doing this will ensure that the submodules are fully coded before the upper-level program structures are finalized.

5. *Coding the main program. After all submodules have been written, write the main program. The purpose of the main program will be sequencing and interfacing the subroutines.*

The imitation approach has some important resemblances to the top-down approach:

1. *The programmer must understand the problem thoroughly before writing code.*

2. *The actual writing of the program is postponed until after certain decisions have been made.*

3. *The problem is broken up into logical units.*

However, there are important different characteristics in the two approaches.

Top-down Approach

1. *In the top-down approach, a specific plan of attack is developed in stages. Only the issues relevant to a given level are considered, and these issues are formalized completely.*

2. *Furthermore, whenever the programmer decides to use a subprogram or procedure, the interfaces (i.e., arguments, returned values, and effects) are decided first. The inputs and outputs are formalized before developing the submodule; that is, the submodules are made to fit the calling routine instead of the other way around.*

3. *Most important, at every step in the top-down approach, the programmer has a complete, correct "program."*

The major disadvantages of the imitation approach are that it is more likely to produce errors, to require major program modifications, or to result in a somewhat ill-conceived program. Choosing a partially specified attack may require serious changes to the program. Coding submodules first may result in a confusing program logic if the submodules do not happen to integrate easily into the upper-level code designed later.

In summary, think carefully about programming technique. The top-down approach, which is discussed at length in Chapter 7, is the smart alternative.

2 STRUCTURE IS LOGIC

❧

"ROSE IS A ROSE IS A ROSE IS A ROSE."

Gertrude Stein
Sacred Emily

*"AN IDEALIST IS ONE WHO, ON NOTICING
THAT A ROSE SMELLS BETTER THAN A
CABBAGE, CONCLUDES THAT IT WILL ALSO
MAKE BETTER SOUP."*

H. L. Mencken
Sententiae

Proverb 8   **CODE IT FOR THE OTHER GUY**

*"Our life is frittered away by detail
. . . Simplify, simplify."*
HENRY DAVID THOREAU
Walden: Where I lived, and what I lived for

Have you ever put together one of those "easily assembled" toys on Christmas eve? The instructions read:

"Attach the tower(B) to the base(A) and the chute(C) to the tower."

In the same manner, the next page of instructions directs:

"The kit contains 16 3/4" bolts. Insert each one into the holes marked "J"; place base(A) snugly so edges(L) are aligned with arrows *inside* base(A). In kit 2, take nuts(D) and . . . ."

and so on, etc. You wonder if the designer of the toy was ever in communication with the author of the instructions on how to put the toy together.

In programming, we have the same problem. Somehow, we get so caught up in design that we forget the user, we forget to code it for the other guy. Eventually, programs work, but that is not the test of a good program. The test is: can a program be easily understood, are there no unnecessary details, and is the logical structure clear? Well-structured programs are the mark of a careful development process and are usually characterized by small, functionally specific modules. Generally, the statements of a Pascal module should not extend beyond one page.

Just like the instructions for assembling the toy, some programmers write calls to procedures like this:

```
READTRANSACTION;
PROCESSTRANSACTION;
UPDATESTATUS;
```

and then you turn to this:

```
procedure UPDATESTATUS;
    -- update data base file with new information
begin
    READ (FIELD.INDICATOR)
    TRANS.COUNT     := 0;
    TRANS.ON        := FALSE;
    TRANS.BUFFSIZE := 100;

    if (FIELD.INDICATOR <> TERMVAL) then
        . . .
        while (STATEVAR = GOVAL) do begin
            HANDLE(NEWTRANS, COUNTER, RESULTSTATUS);
            UPDATETRANSFILE;
            ACOUNT := ACOUNT + 1;
            . . .
        end;
    . . .
end;
```

If you throw your hands up with this, it is understandable. Someone seems to be lying. Why? In this case:

1. *The procedure UPDATESTATUS has probably ten(!) purposes.*

2. *There may be fifteen or so effective inputs or outputs, each buried in the code.*

We need to answer the question: What is a logical structure, and what is a logical unit? It is a section of code, normally a function or procedure with:

1. *a single purpose, and*

2. *clearly stated inputs and outputs.*

Programmers usually violate these two points, and getting to the bottom of such matters is, in a sense, the thrust of this book.

The most direct value of modular code is felt during program maintenance, for time is not wasted trying to determine what is being done over several sections of code. Consider Figure 6a, which outlines the logical structure of a hypothetical program. The structure is difficult to follow. Figure 6b pictures the remedied situation where simple computations are isolated into units.

There are many advantages to modular code. Coding time is shortened by the use of previously written modules. Implementation costs are lower because of easier changes, decreased recompilation costs, smaller tasks, and isolated code bottlenecks. Testing is simpler because "simple" modules usually have not more than, say, a half dozen looping and branching constructs and thus a smaller number of total execution paths. In the end, the dividend is paid in the maintenance of the program.

When the time comes to write the actual code, there are three guidelines that will help you code in logical units:

1. *First, and most obviously, make the best use of functions and procedures.*

2. *Avoid confusing control structures.*

3. *Display the resulting logical structure with good spacing and indentation.*

The next three proverbs treat these issues. But if you think of yourself as the other guy, and simplify, simplify, both the process and the product will be improved.

Figure 6. *Display of logical structure*

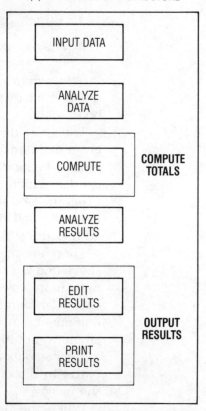

(a) POOR LOGICAL STRUCTURE (b) BETTER LOGICAL STRUCTURE

Proverb 9 *DON'T NEST*

"When I was a ten-year-old girl, my uncle gave me a little Russian doll that looked like an Easter egg. If you turned the head, the egg-doll opened and inside there was another doll until at last, opening the smallest doll, I found a piece of chocolate. But after I had put the dolls back together again, there was no chocolate at the end of my search. I did not under-stand this, although I tried again and again to find the chocolate."

ANONYMOUS

[NOTE: For simplicity of discussion in this proverb, we mention only procedures here. The same, of course, applies to functions.]

A Pascal program consists of:

1. *a sequence of constant, type, and variable declarations followed by*

2. *a sequence of procedure declarations, followed by*

3. *the main program.*

So far, so good.
The hooker comes in the following rule:

4. *a procedure may include declarations of other procedures.*

A procedure declared within another procedure is said to be "nested."
Consider the following, rather common, scenario:

1. *A main program calls a single procedure P.*

2. *The procedure P calls a single procedure Q.*

3. *The procedure Q calls a single procedure R.*

We can write this program as shown in Figure 7(a). Since Q is only used in P, Q is declared within P. Since R is only used in Q, R is declared within Q.

Now, declaring constants, types, and variables within a procedure is an idea strongly recommended. It keeps these items local to the procedure in which they are used, and thus prevents a flooding of the main program with too much information.

But not procedures. Why? They are too big, and they muddle the simple presentation of programs. The program of Figure 7(b) shows the alternative. It is easier to comprehend, and much easier to lay out on the printed page. Imagine the case where P, Q, and R are each a page or two long. How do you print the program in any reasonable manner and still see the overall structure? Practically, this is impossible.

Moral: while nesting dolls is fun, it is not practical to confuse programmers by nesting procedures. Our advice is to skip rule 4 and go with the strategy of Figure 7(b). Don't nest procedures.

Figure 7.   **Nesting**

(a) *How to Use Nesting*

```
program NESTED (INPUT, OUTPUT);
    -- declaration of constants, types, and variables
    -- for the main program

    procedure P;
        -- declarations for P
        procedure Q;
            -- declarations for Q
            procedure R;
                -- declarations for R
            begin
                -- statements of R
            end { R };
        begin
            -- statements of Q
            -- calls R
        end { Q };
    begin
        -- statements of P
        -- calls Q
    end { P };

begin
    -- statements for main program
    -- calls P
end.
```

(b) How to Avoid Nesting

```
program UNNESTED (INPUT, OUTPUT);
    -- declarations of constants, types, and variables
    -- for the main program
procedure R;
    -- declarations for R
begin
    -- statements of R
end { Q };

procedure Q;
    -- declarations for Q
begin
    -- statements of Q
    -- calls R
end { Q };

procedure P;
    -- declarations for P
begin
    -- statements of P
    -- calls Q
end { P };

begin
    -- statements of main program
    -- calls P
end.
```

Proverb 10   ## BLACK-BOX YOUR SUBROUTINES

"Years later, when I was older and my uncle was in the evening of his life, he came to visit and asked about the egg-doll that he had given me. When I brought it to him, I found that the smallest doll had been broken. I was sad. "Do not cry, my child," he said. "But I cannot replace the smallest doll, only the whole doll. Some times, one must replace the whole to repair the part."

ANONYMOUS

The function and procedure facilities in Pascal can be powerful tools for coding clear, modular programs. Not only do these facilities allow the programmer to "factor out" sections of code, but more important, they provide a basic unit for abstraction of program modules. This abstraction can have a great effect on program readability by exposing the program's logical structure, *even if* the function or procedure is called only once.

The basic idea behind procedures and functions is an old and familiar one. We almost grow up with the little equation

```
F(X, Y) -> Z
```

which can also be expressed

This latter view suggests that F is some algorithm expressed in a programming language. Fine, so far.

But when the going gets rough, programmers lose this simple idea. A procedure or function should have all its inputs and outputs identified. Even something like a procedure to update an array should follow the rule, for instance, the array BOARD in

This can be expressed by the procedure header

```
procedure UPDATEBOARD ({for}  PLAYER: COLOR;
                       {using} SQ1, SQ2: SQVALUE;
                       {updating} var BOARD: BOARDCONTENTS);
```

This is the *full* interface for this procedure, no matter how complex its internal algorithm.

Consider the programs of Figure 8. Given the values for the three-element arrays A, B, C, and D, the programs use the determinant method (assuming DENOM is nonzero) to solve three independent equations of the following form of the unknowns x, y, and z:

$$A_1x + B_1y + C_1z = D1$$
$$A_2x + B_2y + C_2z = D2$$
$$A_3x + B_3y + D_3z = D3$$

The program of Figure 8(a) is a confusion of arithmetic calculations. It contains little hint of the determinant method or the algorithm needed to solve the problem. In contrast, Figure 8(b) uses a function subprogram to calculate the determinants. It is explicitly clear that each unknown is the quotient of two determinants and that the denominator is the determinant of the variable coefficient matrix. Figure 8(c) shows an even greater improvement when the arrays are passed as arguments.

There are two points of Figure 8(c): first, by black-boxing subroutines, the entire structure of the program is more logical; second, your program will be longer. But in this fashion, you can use functions and procedures *often*. The other guy can read it more easily, and maintenance and debugging are easier when we can, as with the doll, replace the entire black box rather than tamper with the individual parts.

Figure 8.   *Solution of three independent equations*

(a) Poor Solution: Functions Not Used

```
program EQUATION1 (INPUT, OUTPUT);

    const
        NUMUNKNOWNS = 3;
    type
        COEFFICIENTS = array [1..NUMUNKNOWNS] of REAL;
    var
        A, B, C, D: COEFFICIENTS;
        DENOM:      REAL;
        X, Y, Z:    REAL;
        I:          1..NUMUNKNOWNS;
```

```
begin
   WRITELN ('Enter coefficients: ');
   for I := 1 to NUMUNKNOWNS do
      READLN (A[I], B[I], C[I], D[I]);

   DENOM :=  (A[1]*B[2]*C[3]) + (A[2]*B[3]*C[1]) + (A[3]*B[1]*C[2])
           - (A[3]*B[2]*C[1]) - (A[2]*B[1]*C[3]) - (A[1]*B[3]*C[2]);

   X :=  (D[1]*B[2]*C[3]) + (D[2]*B[3]*C[1]) + (D[3]*B[1]*C[2])
       - (D[3]*B[2]*C[1]) - (D[2]*B[1]*C[3]) - (D[1]*B[3]*C[2]);

   Y :=  (A[1]*D[2]*C[3]) + (A[2]*D[3]*C[1]) + (A[3]*D[1]*C[2])
       - (A[3]*D[2]*C[1]) - (A[2]*D[1]*C[3]) - (A[1]*D[3]*C[2]);

   Z :=  (A[1]*B[2]*D[3]) + (A[2]*B[3]*D[1]) + (A[3]*B[1]*D[2])
       - (A[3]*B[2]*D[1]) - (A[2]*B[1]*D[3]) - (A[1]*B[3]*D[2]);

   X := X / DENOM;
   Y := Y / DENOM;
   Z := Z / DENOM;
   WRITELN ('Unknowns are: ', X, Y, Z)
end.
```

(b) Better Solution: A Function Used

```
program EQUATION 2 (INPUT, OUTPUT);

   const
      NUMUNKNOWNS = 3;
   type
      COEFFICIENTS = array [1..NUMUNKNOWNS] of REAL;
   var
      A, B, C, D: COEFFICIENTS;
      DENOM:      REAL;
      X, Y, Z:    REAL;
      I:          1..NUMUNKNOWNS;

function DETERM(X1,X2,X3, Y1,Y2,Y3, Z1,Z2,Z3: REAL): REAL;
begin
   DETERM :=  (X1*Y2*Z3) + (X2*Y3*Z1) + (X3*Y1*Z2)
            - (X3*Y2*Z1) - (X2*Y1*Z3) - (X1*Y3*Z2)
end;

begin
   WRITELN ('Enter coefficients: ');
   for I := 2 to NUMUNKNOWNS do
      READLN (A[I], B[I], C[I], D[I]);
```

```
    DENOM := DETERM(A[1],B[1],C[1], A[2],B[2],C[2], A[3],B[3],C[3]);

    X := DETERM(D[1],B[1],C[1], D[2],B[2],C[2], D[3],B[3],C[3]);
    Y := DETERM(A[1],D[1],C[1], A[2],D[2],C[2], A[3],D[3],C[3]);
    Z := DETERM(A[1],B[1],D[1], A[2],B[2],D[2], A[3],B[3],D[3]);

    X := X / DENOM;
    Y := Y / DENOM;
    Z := Z / DENOM;
    WRITELN ('Unknowns are: ', X, Y, Z)
end.
```

(c) Still Better Solution:
Using a Function and Passing Arrays

```
program EQUATION3 (INPUT, OUTPUT);

    const
        NUMUNKNOWNS = 3;
    type
        COEFFICIENTS = array [1..NUMUNKNOWNS] of REAL;
    var
        A, B, C, D: COEFFICIENTS;
        DENOM:      REAL;
        X, Y, Z:    REAL;
        I:          1..NUMUNKNOWNS;

function DETERM(R, S, T: COEFFICIENTS): REAL;
begin
    DETERM :=  (R[1]*S[2]*T[3]) + (R[2]*S[3]*T[1]) + (R[3]*S[1]*T[2])
            -  (R[3]*S[2]*T[1]) - (R[2]*S[1]*T[3]) - (R[1]*S[3]*T[2])
end;


begin
    WRITELN ('Enter coefficients: ');
    for I := 1 to NUMUNKNOWNS do
        READLN (A[I], B[I], C[I], D[I]);

    DENOM := DETERM(A, B, C);

    X := DETERM(D, B, C) / DENOM;
    Y := DETERM(A, D, C) / DENOM;
    Z := DETERM(A, B, D) / DENOM;
    WRITELN('Unknowns are: ', X, Y, Z)
end.
```

Proverb 11 *DON'T GOTO*

"A little neglect may breed mischief . . . for want of a nail, the shoe was lost; for want of a shoe, the horse was lost; for want of a horse, the rider was lost."
BENJAMIN FRANKLIN *Maxims, prefixed to Poor Richard's Almanack*

Earlier we observed that program documentation was a controversial issue in programming. But even more controversy has been generated over control structures. What is the best way to ensure that at every point in a program the next action to be carried out will be clearly specified? In many languages, the control structure issue focuses on one small statement: the goto.

The unconditional transfer of control, which is the purpose of the goto statement, has been associated with programming since its inception. Its historical ties have left indelible marks on today's major programming languages. Until recently, virtually all higher-level languages have had some form of an unrestricted goto. My position is this: make a little sign and hang it where you can see it every day:

DO NOT GOTO

YOU DON'T HAVE TO

Let me show you why. Consider the following little example.

```
SUM   := 0;
COUNT := 0;

10: if (COUNT > MAX) then
        goto 20;
    SUM   := SUM + COUNT;
    COUNT := COUNT + 2;
    goto 10;
20: WRITELN (SUM);
```

This is hardly complex, but does make the point. The goto's force us to develop a mental image of chasing about. This disappears with the alternative rendering:

```
SUM   := 0;
COUNT := 0;
while COUNT <= MAX do begin
   SUM   := SUM + COUNT;
   COUNT := COUNT + 2
end;
WRITELN (SUM)
```

Moreover, it is now really clear that the program contains a single loop, and when the loop is complete, COUNT is greater than MAX.

In another setting, consider the two programs of Figure 9. Here we see simple subroutines for finding an occurrence of a substring (designated by two character positions) in a given source string. Under certain conditions, the subroutine sets an error flag.

In particular, both segments of code perform the following computation.

Inputs:

SOURCESTR:	a string of characters
STRLENGTH:	the length of the string
POS1, POS2:	the start and end positions of a substring

Outputs:

SUBSTR:	the substring of SOURCESTR from POS1 to POS2
ERROR:	FALSE if (POS1 < POS2 < STRLENGTH);
	TRUE otherwise

Here the type

```
STRING = packed array [1..100] of CHAR;
```

is assumed. Also, if ERROR is true, no value is assigned to SUBSTR.

In Figure 9(a), we see a quite tightly nested series of interconnected if statements. In Figure 9(b), we have a program derived from the use of alternative control structures. The second example provides a much clearer description of the algorithm, mainly because of the use of simple 1-in, 1-out control structures.

The differences between these two programs are quite clearly expressed in their corresponding flowcharts, shown in Figures 10 and 11. In the first illustration, the flowchart shows a profusion of branching lines; in the second, a clearer structure is evident.

In yet another setting, consider the program segments of Figure 12. These segments employ a variation of the bubble sort algorithm to sort an array A, containing 500 entries. The array A is declared of type

```
array[1..50] of REAL;
```

The subroutine SWAP exchanges the values of the two variables given as arguments. Basically, the programs scan the array A once from the top (position 1) to the bottom (position 500). At each examined position in the array, the elements at the top of the position are already in order, and the program checks to see if the element in the next position is itself in order. If not, the element is swapped with the previous element and then "bubbled" up until its proper place in the sorted part of the array is found. Processing then continues at the position below the element originally examined.

One point of this example is that the (possibly) small gain in efficiency via the goto is not as important as the improvement in clarity when the programmer uses alternative ways of constructing his program.

The trap that programmers fall into is trying to "get rid" of goto's. If you play that game, the secret to winning is to start from the problem. Someone says, "Hey, this goto is perfect."

```
while (I < J) do begin
    ...
    if (X < Y) then
        begin
            ...
            goto 999;
            ...
        end
    ...
    end;
    ...
999: DOSOMETHING;
```

You are at a loss. But, just start over, from the problem. Try to undo the logic that led to this deeply embedded goto. The name of the real game is to *program without* goto's. The reason is to *force* a clear, sensible logic to all your code.

Figure 9.   ***Control structures***

(a) Poor

```
if (POS1 <= 0) then
  goto 10
else
  goto 15;

10: ERROR := TRUE;
    goto 40;

15: if (POS2 < POS1) or (POS2 > 100) then
      goto 10
    else
      goto 20;

20:  if (POS2 - POS1) > STRLENGTH then
        goto 10
     else
        goto 30;

30:  ERROR := FALSE;
     for I := POS1 to POS2 do begin
        CHARPOS := (I - POS1) + 1;
        SUBSTR[CHARPOS] := SOURCESTR[I]
     end;

40:  {return}
```

(b) Better

```
if (POS1 <= 0) or (POS2 < POS1) or (POS2 > 100)
or (POS2 - POS1 > STRLENGTH) then
   ERROR := TRUE
else
   begin
      ERROR := FALSE;
      for I := POS1 to POS2 do begin
         CHARPOS := (I - POS1) + 1;
         SUBSTR[CHARPOS] := SOURCESTR[I]
      end
   end
```

Figure 10.   **Flowchart for Figure 9a**

Figure 11.   *Flowchart for Figure 9b*

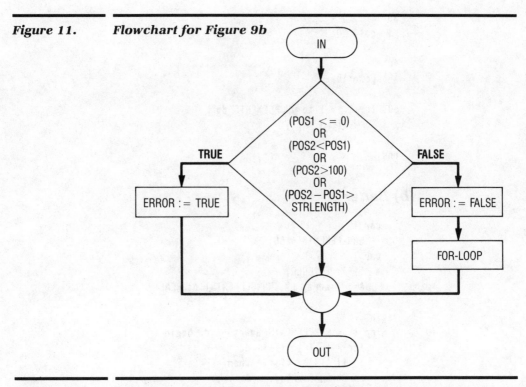

Figure 12.   *A variant of the bubble sort algorithm*

(a) Poor

```
label
    10, 20, 30, 40, 50;
const
    NUMELEMENTS = 50;
var
    I, J: INTEGER;
    A:    array [1..NUMELEMENTS] of REAL;

begin
    I := NUMELEMENTS;
10: if I = 1 then
        goto 50;
    J := 1;

20: if J = I then
        goto 40;
    if A[J] <= A[J+1] then
        goto 30;
    SWAP (A[J], A[J+1]);
```

```
30: J := J + 1;
    goto 20;

40: I := I - 1;
    goto 10;

50: for I := 1 to NUMELEMENTS do
        WRITELN (A[I])

end;
```

(b) Better

```
const
    NUMELEMENTS = 50;
var
    I, J: INTEGER;
    A:    array [1..NUMELEMENTS] of REAL;

begin
    for I := NUMELEMENTS downto 2 do begin
        for J := 1 to (I-1) do
            if A[J] > A[J+1] then
                SWAP (A[J], A[J+1]);
    end;

    for I := 1 to NUMELEMENTS do
        WRITELN (A[I])
end;
```

In summary, the deeper issue here is not merely the elimination of goto's but the use of a clear, logical program structure. The trouble with goto's is that when they are abused, they can lead a programmer down the path of a confusing, almost spaghetti-like, logic. Chapter 5, which discusses Pascal program standards, provides specific rules for the use of well-formed control structures. If you stick to these standards *from the beginning*, the goto problem may go away.

As in all four proverbs of this section, the deeper issue here is not the elimination of goto's, nesting, or black-boxing: it is coding in logical structure so the other guy can read it.

3

CODING THE PROGRAM

❧

"WORKS DONE LEAST RAPIDLY, ART MOST CHERISHES."

Robert Browning
Old Pictures in Florence, Stanza 17

Proverb 12 | ***ALL WORDS MEAN SOMETHING***

"When I use a word," Humpty Dumpty said, in a rather scornful tone, "it means just what I choose it to mean—neither more nor less." "The question is," Alice said, "whether you can make words mean so many different things."
LEWIS CARROLL
Alice Through the Looking Glass

The adjective "mnemonic" is a useful modifier for programmers, especially in Pascal, where precision in choosing words is necessary. It means " . . . assisting or intending to assist the memory." As it is difficult to overestimate the value of using mnemonic, user-defined names, it is also easy to become careless using names that may later complicate or confuse the intent of a program. Principles for selecting good mnemonic names are discussed at length in Chapter 4. Here it is sufficient to make one point: use names that correctly reflect the objects they are intended to represent.

The disadvantage of poor names is easily seen in Figure 13. The programmer who writes code like the code shown in Figure 13(a) will probably need to keep a separate list specifying what each variable name represents. Otherwise the programmer may lose track of what each variable does. Figure 13(b) significantly clarifies the situation. The names themselves almost state the intended calculation.

Figure 13(b), however, is written using variable names with a maximum length of six characters (the requirement in standard Fortran). Figure 13(c) shows the possibilities in Pascal, and Figure 13(d) illustrates the possibilities in languages like PL/I that allow break characters within names. Certainly OVERTIMEWAGE and OVERTIME__WAGE are more informative than OVTIME.

The challenge in picking names is somehow to balance the following criteria:

1. *Accuracy*

2. *Brevity*

3. *Spurious effects*

For instance, consider Figure 14(a). The names here might appear fine at first glance. But look at these problems.

SUITNUM	*it is not a variable, as suggested by the name.*
D	*too short for a major name.*
INDEX	*too long for an innocent count.*
COUNTS	*the plural is odd.*
SVAL	*cryptic.*

These problems are rectified in Figure 14(b).

These examples indicate that the thoughtful use of mnemonic names improves the readability for the programmer and for those who read the program later. It is worth the time to devise and use informative names. You may not fully appreciate the benefits of your efforts now, but you will when a large program has to be debugged or modified later. Then you will appreciate that you chose a word to mean exactly what you wanted to mean. Mnemonic assistance is then priceless.

Figure 13. *Use of mnemonic names*

(a) Poor (BASIC revisited)

```
LET G = (W * H) + (O * X)
LET T = R1 * G
LET S = S1 * G
LET P = G - T - S
```

(b) Better (FORTRAN revisited)

```
GROSS = (WAGE * HOURS) + (OVTIME * XHOURS)
TAX   = TAXRATE * GROSS
SSEC  = SSRATE * GROSS
PAY   = GROSS - TAX - SSEC
```

(c) Best (good use of Pascal)

```
GROSSPAY     := (WAGE * HOURS) + (OVERTIMEWAGE * EXTRAHOURS);
TAX          := TAXRATE * GROSSPAY;
SOCSECURITY  := SOCSECRATE * GROSSPAY;
NETPAY       := GROSSPAY - TAX - SOCSECURITY;
```

(d) The PL/I option

```
GROSS_PAY     = (WAGE * HOURS) + (OVERTIME_WAGE * EXTRA_HOURS);
TAX           = TAX_RATE * GROSS_PAY;
SOC_SECURITY  = SOC_SEC_RATE * GROSS_PAY;
NET_PAY       = GROSS_PAY - TAX - SOC_SECURITY;
```

Figure 14. *Use of mnemonic names*

(a) Paying token homage

```
const
    SUITNUM = 4;
    RANKNUM = 13;
    CARDNUM = 51;
    DECKNUM = 52:

type
    CARD = record
              SVAL: 1..SUITNUM;
              RVAL: 1..RANKNUM
           end;
    NAME = packed array [1..5] of CHAR;
    RANK = array [1..RANKNUM] of INTEGER;
    DECK = array [1..DECKNUM] of CARD;
```

49

```
procedure PRINTCARD (D: DECK);

{ -- This procedure examines a deck of cards with one missing
  -- card. It finds and prints the rank (e.g., "THREE" or
  -- "KING") of the missing card. }

    var
        COUNTS:  RANK;
        NAMESTR: NAME;
        RANKVAL: INTEGER;
        INDEX:   INTEGER;

begin
    for RANKVAL := 1 to RANKNUM do
        COUNTS[RANKVAL] := 0;

    for INDEX := 1 to CARDNUM do begin
        RANKVAL := D[INDEX].RVAL;
        COUNTS[RANKVAL] := COUNTS[RANKVAL] + 1
    end;

    for RANKVAL := 1 to RANKNUM do
        if COUNTS[RANKVAL] < SUITNUM then
            NAMESTR := RANKNUM(RANKVAL);
    WRITELN ('Missing rank: ', NAMESTR)
end;
```

(b) More accurate names

```
const
    NUMSUITS = 4;
    NUMRANKS = 13;
    NUMCARDS = 51;
    DECKSIZE = 52;

type
    CARDINFO     = record
                       SUITVAL: 1..NUMSUITS;
                       RANKVAL: 1..NUMRANKS
                   end;
    RANKNAME     = packed array [1..5] of CHAR;
    RANKTALLY    = array [1..NUMRANKS] of INTEGER;
    DECKCONTENTS = array [1..DECKSIZE] of CARDINFO;
```

```
procedure FINDMISSINGCARD (DECK: DECKCONTENTS);

{ -- This procedure examines a deck of cards with one missing
  -- card. It finds and prints the rank (e.g., "THREE" or
  -- "KING") of the missing card. }

    var
        COUNT: RANKTALLY ;
        NAME:  RANKNAME ;
        RANK:  INTEGER;
        I:     INTEGER;

begin
    for RANK := 1 to NUMRANKS do
        COUNT[RANK] := 0;

    for I := 1 to NUMCARDS do begin
        RANK := DECK[I].RANKVAL;
        COUNT[RANK] := COUNT[RANK] + 1
    end;

    for RANK := 1 to NUMRANKS do
        if COUNT[RANK] < NUMSUITS then
            NAME := RANKNAME[RANK];
    WRITELN ('Missing rank: ', NAME)
end;
```

Proverb 13   *SPACES HAVE*   *"Well timed silence hath more*
              MEANING, TOO   *eloquence than speech."*
                                      MARTIN FARQUAHAR TUPPER
                                      Of Discretion

Somewhere, in some graduate student class, a term was coined that may seem trite but, as in the previous proverb, means something: "prettyprinting." Briefly defined, it means the effective use of "extra" spaces, blank lines, or special characters to delineate the logical structure of a program.

Prettyprinting is especially useful in the verification and maintenance of programs. It helps to detect errors, such as improperly structured data description entries and incorrectly nested if statements. Furthermore, a programmer trying to read the program does not have to devote extra time to discovering its structure, an advantage that makes the program considerably easier to understand.

At the "macro" level, the goal of prettyprinting is to show the logical structure of major program units. For instance, suppose we have a program of the form

1. *program header*

2. *half page of comments*

3. *half page of declarations*

4. *a one-page procedure ALPHA*

5. *a two-page procedure BETA*

6. *a thirty-line main program.*

If this is the structure, then prettyprinting means showing it, not leaving it to the reader to figure it out. The key here is to use page breaks between major units, as shown in Figure 15.

Obvious? Sure, but take a peek at a professional program sometime and see how often it is done.

At the "mini" level, the goal is to show the logical units of a single module. For instance, consider

```
ACOUNT := 0;
ECOUNT := 0;
ICOUNT := 0;
OCOUNT := 0;
UCOUNT := 0;
while not EOF do begin
   -- body of loop
end;
```

There *should* be (it is not a matter of "taste") one blank line here. Where? Just before the while loop. Why? Because there

Figure 15.   ***Displaying overall structure with page breaks***

```
program SHOWME;
    -- comments describing
    -- the program
    . . .
    -- and ending here
```

```
type
    type declarations
var
    variable declarations
```

```
procedure ALPHA;
    declarations
begin
    statements
end;
```

```
procedure BETA;
    declarations
begin
    statements
end;
```

```
begin
    statements for main program
end.
```

----

are two logical units: (a) initialization of counters and (b) a processing loop. It is impossible to give hard and fast rules where to put blank lines, but the gist of it is

** between conceptual chunks

Some programmers stuff a few blank lines in just for looks, but the purpose is to show *meaning*.

At the "micro" level, the goal is to show the individual parts of statements. You would be horrified to see

```
ACOUNT:=ACOUNT     +    1   ;
```

but not

```
ACOUNT := ACOUNT + 1;
```

The reason is that the correct spacing illuminates the correct meaning.

There are all kinds of cases where a little white space is effective. Consider

```
(a)   ACCOUNT:=0

(b)   T+R*Q

(c)   WRITE('A =',ACCOUNT)

(d)   DECK=array[1..52]of CARD;

(e)   if HEIGHT<STANDARD then ...

(f)   WRITE(I:5,J:5)

(g)   CARDVALUE[RANK]+1

(h)   F(X/2.0,Y/2.0,Z/2.0)

(i)   (SUNDAY,MONDAY,TUESDAY)
```

These can all be improved:

```
(a)   ACCOUNT := 0                    {-- shows the two sides}

(b)   T + R*Q                         {-- shows precedence}
```

```
(c)   WRITE ('A'= ', ACOUNT)          {-- shows two arguments}

(d)   DECK = array [1..52] of CARD    {-- shows names vs. definition}

(e)   if HEIGHT < STANDARD then ...   {-- not so crammed}

(f)   WRITE (I:5, J:5)                {-- colon has higher precedence}

(g)   CARDVALUE[RANK] + 1             {-- shows two sides of plus}

(h)   F(X/2.0, Y/2.0, Z/2.0)          {-- shows three arguments}

(i)   (SUNDAY, MONDAY, TUESDAY)       {-- shows three values}
```

Again, the same point: *Meaning, Meaning, Meaning!* Yet, professional programmers, students, and authors often miss the point and treat spacing as a second-class issue.

As an example, four complete Pascal programs are listed in Figures 16(a) through 16(d). The first three are not well prettyprinted; the last shows careful thought in prettyprinting. Even in some textbooks, uses of Pascal are seldom exposed to the full potential of prettyprinting, although almost every implementation admits great latitude in the spacing of programs.

In our examples, we have attempted to incorporate certain prettyprinting examples. Appendix A itemizes some of these standards; they are the product of many revisions and should be useful to all Pascal programmers. We encourage the reader to make use of these standards. But keep in mind that standards (and automatic prettyprinting programs) only provide a minimum guide. It's the meaning that counts, both in the words and in the spaces. If the program you are writing has a good logical structure, then show it.

Figure 16.   *Prettyprinting*

(a) Lack of prettyprinting

```
program VOWELS(INPUT,OUTPUT);
var CHARACTER:CHAR; ACOUNT, ECOUNT,
ICOUNT, OCOUNT, UCOUNT: INTEGER;
```

```
begin ACOUNT := 0;
ECOUNT := 0;  ICOUNT := 0;
OCOUNT := 0;  UCOUNT := 0;
WRITELN ('Enter line of text:');

while not EOLN do begin READ(CHARACTER);
if CHARACTER in ['A', 'E', 'I', 'O', 'U'] then
    case CHARACTER of
    'A':ACOUNT:=ACOUNT+1;
    'E':ECOUNT:=ECOUNT+1;
    'I':ICOUNT:=ICOUNT+1;
    'O':OCOUNT:=OCOUNT+1;
    'U':UCOUNT:=UCOUNT+1 end end;
WRITELN(' A = ',ACOUNT:1,' E= ',ECOUNT:1,' I = ',ICOUNT:1,'
' O = ',OCOUNT:1, ' U = ',UCOUNT:1)
end.
```

(b) Giving token thought to prettyprinting

```
program VOWELS(INPUT, OUTPUT);
var CHARACTER: CHAR;
    ACOUNT, ECOUNT, ICOUNT, OCOUNT, UCOUNT: INTEGER;
begin
ACOUNT:=0;
ECOUNT:=0;
ICOUNT:=0;
OCOUNT:=0;
UCOUNT:=0;

WRITELN ('Enter line of text:');

while not EOLN do begin
READ (CHARACTER);
if CHARACTER in ['A','E','I','O','U'] then
    case CHARACTER of
        'A': ACOUNT := ACOUNT+1;
        'E': ECOUNT := ECOUNT+1;
        'I': ICOUNT := ICOUNT+1;
        'O': OCOUNT := OCOUNT+1;
        'U': UCOUNT := UCOUNT+1
    end
end;
WRITELN(' A=',ACOUNT:1, ' E=',ECOUNT:1, ' I=',ICOUNT:1, ' O=',OCOUNT:1,
    ' U=',UCOUNT:1)
end.
```

(c) *Going overboard*

```
program VOWELS ( INPUT , OUTPUT );
var

    CHARACTER : CHAR;

    ACOUNT,
    ECOUNT,
    ICOUNT,
    OCOUNT,
    UCOUNT : INTEGER;

begin

    ACOUNT  :=  0;
    ECOUNT  :=  0;
    ICOUNT  :=  0;
    OCOUNT  :=  0;
    UCOUNT  :=  0;
    WRITELN ('Enter line of text:');
    while not EOLN do

        begin

            READ  ( CHARACTER );

            if CHARACTER in [ 'A',  'E;',  'I',  'O',  'U' ]
               then

                    case CHARACTER of

                            'A' :   ACOUNT := ACOUNT + 1;
                            'E' :   ECOUNT := ECOUNT + 1;
                            'I' :   ICOUNT := ICOUNT + 1;
                            'O' :   OCOUNT := OCOUNT + 1;
                            'U' :   UCOUNT := UCOUNT + 1

                    end
        end;

    WRITELN( ' A = ',   ACOUNT:1,
             ' E = ',   ECOUNT:1,
             ' I = ',   ICOUNT:1,
             ' O = ',   OCOUNT:1,
             ' U = ',   UCOUNT:1 )

end.
```

(d) Good prettyprinting

```pascal
program VOWELS (INPUT, OUTPUT);
    var
        CHARACTER: CHAR;
        ACOUNT, ECOUNT, ICOUNT,
        OCOUNT, UCOUNT: INTEGER;

begin
    ACOUNT := 0;
    ECOUNT := 0;
    ICOUNT := 0;
    OCOUNT := 0;
    UCOUNT := 0;

    WRITELN ('Enter line of text:');
    while not EOLN do begin
        READ (CHARACTER);
        if CHARACTER in ['A', 'E', 'I', 'O', 'U'] then
            case CHARACTER of
                'A': ACOUNT := ACOUNT + 1;
                'E': ECOUNT := ECOUNT + 1;
                'I': ICOUNT := ICOUNT + 1;
                'O': OCOUNT := OCOUNT + 1;
                'U': UCOUNT := UCOUNT + 1
            end
    end;

    WRITELN (' A = ', ACOUNT:1,  ' E = ', ECOUNT:1,
             ' I = ', ICOUNT:1,  ' O = ', OCOUNT:1, ' U = ', UCOUNT:1);

end.
```

Proverb 14   **COMMENT FOR CONTENT**

"And none can read the text, not even I; And none can read the comment but myself."
ALFRED, LORD TENNYSON
Pelleas and Ettarre

What the poet has to say above is, unfortunately, all too descriptive of too many programs written today. The myths surrounding the use of comments in programs is perhaps dispelled in this simple test:

True or false:	A readable program is one with copious comments.
Answer:	Usually, false.
True or false:	A good program may have no comments in the statement part.
Answer:	Possibly, true.

Comments are a form of internal documentation that allows the programmer to describe the internal workings of a program. One example will suffice to make the point. Consider the program of Figure 17(a). This program has no comments. The reader is invited to examine the program and determine the meaning of each statement.

Next consider the program of Figure 17(b). The comments convey the logical structure of the program. O.K. But they go too far. They are distracting and tell the obvious.

Figure 17(c) shows a deeper concern for the reader. The comments are clearly separated from the code and give more precise statements about the entire function, even telling us about Euclid's algorithms.

Although the value of using comments can be illustrated over and over again, the programmer is often tempted not to use them. After all, when a programmer is writing a piece of code, comments may not be needed. But how many times during coding does the programmer go back to try to figure out what has happened and what is left to do? And what about the next day? Or the next week? Or the occasion when you are asked to change someone else's program?

One additional proverb is useful here: *Temperance is moderation in all things*. Comments can be overused as well as misused. It is far better to use good prettyprinting and good mnemonic names rather than to clutter up your code with copious comments. Comments should convey useful information. Frequent comments like

```
{ -- A gets B plus C }
    A := B + C;
```

not only clutter up your program but may completely discourage anyone from trying to wade through it.

Here are Henry's three rules for Pascal comments:

1. *Write header comments (for the main program, a proce-dure, or a function).*

2. *Do header comments before coding.*

3. *Try not to use any other comments.*

Don't let rule 3 confuse you. Good code speaks for itself: if a piece of code needs a comment, it is likely that the code itself could be better.

In short, comments can promote the design of maintainable programs. They can make a difference. *Use them, temperately.*

Figure 17.   ***Use of effective comments***
                  (a) Poor solution: no comments

```
program GCD1 (INPUT, OUTPUT);
    var
        HIVALUE, LOVALUE, REMAINDER: INTEGER;
        GCD, N1, N2: INTEGER;

begin
    WRITE ('Enter two positive integers: ');
    READ (N1, N2);
    if N1 <= N2 then
        begin
            LOVALUE := N1;
            HIVALUE := N2
        end
    else
        begin
            LOVALUE := N2;
            HIVALUE := N1
        end;

    repeat
        REMAINDER := HIVALUE mod LOVALUE;
        HIVALUE := LOVALUE;
        LOVALUE := REMAINDER
    until REMAINDER = 0;

    GCD := HIVALUE;
    WRITE ('GCD is ', GCD)
end.
```

(b) Poor solution: overdoing it

```
program GCD2 (INPUT, OUTPUT);

{ Function to compute the greatest common divisor of
  two numbers using Euclid's algorithm. Euclid's algorithm
  is one of repeated division. }

    var
        HIVALUE, LOVALUE, REMAINDER: INTEGER;
        GCD, N1, N2: INTEGER;


begin
   { Get initial values. }

   WRITE ('Enter two positive integers: ');
   READ (N1, N2);


   { Place in order. }
   if N1 <= N2 then
      begin
         LOVALUE := N1;
         HIVALUE := N2
      end
   else
      begin
         LOVALUE := N2;
         HIVALUE := N1
      end;


   { Perform Euclid's algorithm until GCD is found. }
   repeat
      REMAINDER := HIVALUE mod LOVALUE;
      HIVALUE := LOVALUE;
      LOVALUE := REMAINDER
   until REMAINDER = 0;


   { Print results. }
   GCD := HIVALUE;
   WRITE ('GCD is ', GCD)
end.
```

(c) Best solution: careful commenting

```pascal
program GCD3 (INPUT, OUTPUT);

{ -- Euclid's algorithm for the greatest common divisor:
  --    (1) The larger number is divided by the smaller.
  --    (2) If the remainder is nonzero, it becomes the next divisor
  --        and the original divisor becomes the next dividend.
  --    (3) If zero, the current divisor is the GCD. }

  var
      HIVALUE, LOVALUE, REMAINDER: INTEGER;
      GCD, N1, N2: INTEGER;

begin
    WRITE ('Enter two positive integers: ');
    READ (N1, N2);
    if N1 <= N2 then
        begin
            LOVALUE := N1;
            HIVALUE := N2
        end
    else
        begin
            LOVALUE := N2;
            HIVALUE := N1
        end;

    repeat
        REMAINDER := HIVALUE mod LOVALUE;
        HIVALUE := LOVALUE;
        LOVALUE := REMAINDER
    until REMAINDER = 0;

    GCD := HIVALUE;
    WRITE ('GCD is ', GCD)
end.
```

Proverb 15   *Make Constants Constant*

The result of this proverb is most valuable after a program is written, in other words, during program testing or maintenance. The essential idea is to make sure that all constant data items are recognized and given a value in a constant declaration. Furthermore, no executable statement should modify these constant data items.

Consider the programming situation of Figure 18(a). The programmer assumed that the table would always contain 50 items. The integer 50, besides its use in constructing tables, was used freely throughout the programs in computing averages and controlling conditions. When an increase in data items resulted in 100 items, changing the number 50 to 100 was a searching chore, it was all too easy to miss an occurrence of the integer 50. This is not the case with Figure 18(b), where a data name was created and given a value in the constant declaration.

Not all numbers should be named. Consider the simple code fragments of Figure 19. Here the gain is not clear. Reason? The conversion factor 9/5 and the base 32 stand for themselves.

The real issue involved here concerns the so-called "magic numbers," numbers such as those used in Figure 20(a). How many times while reading code have you been stumped by what 75 and 124.0 are all about? A preceding comment line might help, but isn't the alternative of Figure 20(b) much better?

The principle is this:

• If a number, character, or string has a meaning that is not self-apparent, might be changed, or is confusing on its own, name it.

Figure 18. **Integer constants**

(a) Poor

```
var
    AVERAGE,
    TOTAL: REAL;
    I    : INTEGER;
    LIST : array [1..50] of REAL;
begin
    ...
    TOTAL := 0;
    for INDEX := 1 to 50 do
        TOTAL := TOTAL + LIST[I];
    AVERAGE := TOTAL / 50;
    ...
    for I := 1 to 50 do
        WRITE (LIST[I]);
    WRITELN;
    WRITELN ('Average value = ', AVERAGE);
    ...
end;
```

(b) Better

```
const
    NUMITEMS = 50;
var
    AVERAGE,
    TOTAL: REAL;
    I    : INTEGER;
    LIST : array [1..NUMITEMS] of REAL;
begin
    ...
    TOTAL := 0;
    for I := 1 to NUMITEMS do
        TOTAL := TOTAL * LIST[I];
    AVERAGE := TOTAL / NUMITEMS;
    ...
    for I := 1 to NUMITEMS do
        WRITE (LIST[I];
    WRITELN;
    WRITELN ('Average value = ', AVERAGE);
    ...
end;
```

Figure 19.   *Naming obvious constants*

(a) One way

```
function CENTIGRADE(FARENHEIT: REAL): REAL;
begin
    CENTIGRADE := (9/5)*(FARENHEIT - 32)
end;
```

(b) Better?—No

```
function CENTIGRADE(FARENHEIT: REAL): REAL;
    const
        CONVFACTOR = 1.8;
        BASEFACTOR = 32;

begin
    CENTIGRADE := CONVFACTOR*(FARENHEIT - BASEVALUE)
end;
```

Figure 20.   ***Magic numbers***

(a) Poor

```
function WEIGHTCHECK(HEIGHT, WEIGHT: REAL): WEIGHTSTATUS;
{ -- Function to determine if a man's weight lies within
  -- normal limits. For heights from 62 to 75 inches.
  --
  -- On exit, WEIGHTCHECK returns one of:
  --    TOOSHORT, TOOTALL, OVERWEIGHT, UNDERWEIGHT, NORMAL }

begin
    if HEIGHT < 62.0 then
        WEIGHTCHECK := TOOSHORT
    else if HEIGHT > 75.0 then
        WEIGHTCHECK := TOOTALL
    else if WEIGHT > (133.0 + 4.3*(HEIGHT - 62.0)) then
        WEIGHTCHECK := OVERWEIGHT
    else if WEIGHT < (124.0 + 4.0*(HEIGHT - 62.0)) then
        WEIGHTCHECK := UNDERWEIGHT
    else
        WEIGHTCHECK := NORMAL
end;
```

(b) Better

```
function WEIGHTCHECK(HEIGHT, WEIGHT: REAL): WEIGHTSTATUS;
{ -- Function to determine whether a man's weight lies within
  -- normal limits. For heights from 62 to 75 inches.
  --
  -- On exit, WEIGHTCHECK returns one of:
  --    TOOSHORT, TOOTALL, OVERWEIGHT, UNDERWEIGHT, NORMAL }
   const
      MINHEIGHT = 62.0;
      MAXHEIGHT = 75.0;
      LOWEIGHT  = 124.0;
      HIWEIGHT  = 133.0;
      CONVFAC1  = 4.3;
      CONVFAC2  = 4.0;
begin
   if HEIGHT < MINHEIGHT then
      WEIGHTCHECK := TOOSHORT
   else if HEIGHT > MAXHEIGHT then
      WEIGHTCHECK := TOOTALL
   else if WEIGHT > (HIWEIGHT + CONVFAC1*(HEIGHT - MINHEIGHT)) then
      WEIGHTCHECK := OVERWEIGHT
   else if WEIGHT < (LOWEIGHT + CONVFAC2*(HEIGHT - MINHEIGHT)) then
      WEIGHTCHECK := UNDERWEIGHT
   else
      WEIGHTCHECK := NORMAL
end;
```

Thus, we should have constant declarations like

```
const
   SOCSECRATE    = 12.45;
   NUMITEMS      = 50;
   MAXLINELENGTH = 80;
   STDINDENT     = 10;
   CONTROLCHAR   = '@';
   BLANK         = ' ';
   FILLER        = '        ';
   MARKER        = '**';
```

On the other hand, there will be a few (only a few) cases where a constant can stand on its own; for instance,

> 52   *the number of cards in a deck.*

> 9/5   *farenheit to centigrade conversion factor.*

> 0   *initial value of a sum.*

Here, you have a choice, name it or not. (But don't name it 0.)

Perhaps Shakespeare's remark in one of his sonnets summarizes this proverb better: "A constant is a wonderous excellence." The moral is simple: a well-designed program isolates constant data items in a constant declaration. There are two advantages. First, program modification is easier. But more important, reading the program is not an exercise in detective work, i.e., it is not supposed to be a mystery for the reader. You will need more constant declarations, but this is a small, one-time price to pay for the long-term dividend of a logically organized program.

Proverb 16   *NAME ALL TYPES*

> *"There are ways, but the Way is uncharted; There are names but not nature in words: Nameless indeed is the source of creation But things have a mother and she has a name."*
> LAO TZU *The Way of Life, I*

What is an unnamed type? Look at the following:

```
type
    CARDDECK = array [1..52] of record
                                SUIT: INTEGER;
                                RANK: INTEGER
                            end;


var
    A: array [1..NUMTESTS] of REAL;
    D: CARDDECK;
```

For the variable A, what is the *name* of its type? There is none. For D[2], what is its *name* of the type? There is none. Both have unnamed types.

Now consider the following:

```
type
    CARDINFO = record
                SUIT: INTEGER;
                RANK: INTEGER
            end
```

67

```
CARDDECK = array [1..52] of CARDINFO;
TESTRESULTS = array [1..NUMTESTS] of REAL;

var
    A: TESTRESULTS;
    D: CARDDECK;
```

What is the name of type of A? TESTRESULTS. What is the name of type of D[2]? CARDINFO. Both now have named types.

Why should we name all types?

1. *It is an easy thing to do.*

2. *Procedure and function parameters must have named types.*

3. *The name tells us what the type means.*

Why is this proverb lost on most programmers? Maybe they haven't thought about it, maybe it takes a little extra effort.

It's a good idea. Try it.

Proverb 17   *GET THE SYNTAX CORRECT NOW*

"Experience is the name everyone gives to their mistakes."
OSCAR WILDE Lady Windemere's Fan, Act III

In Pascal, there is a great deal of criticism about its highly sensitive syntax and much of that criticism is often passed on to a Pascal compiler for not helping to add "trivial" missing spaces, commas, or lines.

Consider the program fragments of Figure 21(a), which contain such trivial syntactic errors. Figure 21(b) shows the corresponding corrected version. (Note: In implementations that relax some of the requirements of standard Pascal, some of the constructs in Figure 21(a) are acceptable.)

Errors like the ones in the first example should be screened out in advance by a careful programmer. It is our contention that no errors, no matter how trivial, should pass the attention of a good programmer, for it is possible that some of them may not be detected by the compiler and will appear only after a program is in full operation.

Figure 21.   ***Some simple syntactic errors***

(a) Wrong

```
1.   X = X + 1;

2.   var INDEX = INTEGER;

3.   for I = 1, N do

4.   X = ((Y*Z) + (C/D) / 4

5.   procedure SORT(NAME: array [1..50] of REAL);

6.   procedure SQUARE(A, Y: REAL);
     begin
        Y := A**2
     end.

7.   var X, Y, Z: REAL;
     Z := X div Y;

8.   if A <> 0.0 then
         X1 := B + (SQRT((B*B) - (4*A*C)) / (2*A));
         X2 := B - (SQRT((B*B) - (4*A*C)) / (2*A))
     else
         X1 := -C / B
         X2 := 0.0;

9.   WRITELN ('A poorly structured program is like a syntax, error);

10.  cons
         PI = 3.14159;
     var
         I: INTEGER;


         SUB   := SUM + TEMP
       end;
     PI := SQRT(SQRT(DELTA*SUM));
```

(b) Correct

```
1.   X := X + 1;

2.   var INDEX: INTEGER;

3.   for I := 1 to N do

4.   X := ((Y*Z) + (C/D)) / 4;

5.   procedure SORT(NAME: NAMESTRING);

6.   procedure SQUARE(A: REAL; var Y: REAL);
     begin
        Y := A*A
     end;

7.   var X, Y, Z: REAL;
     if Y <> 0 then
        Z := X / Y
     else
        WRITELN (' ATTEMPT TO DIVIDE BY ZERO!')

8.   if A <> 0.0 then
        begin
           X1 := B + (SQRT((B*B) - (4*A(C)) / (2*A));
           X2 := B - (SQRT((B*B) - (4*A(C)) / (2*A))
        end
     else
        begin
           X1 := -C / B;
           X2 := 0.0
        end;

9.   WRITELN ('A poorly structured program is like a syntax error');

10.  const
        PI = 3.14159;
     var
        I: INTEGER;
```

Sometimes we work away at a program on our desk and the manual for syntax is out in the car. Rather than pause for a moment to ensure that a particular syntactic construction is correct, we press forward thinking that any trivial error will be caught during verification of the program. Not so. The time to consider syntax is not while verifying the completed program but while preparing it. Keep the manual or composite language skeleton handy as you write the code. If you are not absolutely positive that the syntax of the statement you are writing is perfect, look it up. It only takes a few seconds, and your grasp of the language will improve with constant references to the manual. This work habit is all the more crucial if you are just learning Pascal or if you have done considerable programming in another language with similar but nevertheless different syntactic constructs.

You can and should write programs that are completely free of syntactic errors on the first run. But to do so, you have to be convinced that you can indeed do it. Have someone else read the work you produce (Proverb 22). Just think of all the hours of turnaround time that are wasted tracking down simple syntactic errors, not to mention some severe run-time problems that can be caused by such "trivial" errors.

Proverb 18	***REMEMBER YOUR READER***	*"Whenever you teach, be brief, that your readers' minds may readily comprehend and faithfully retain your words."* HORACE Epistles, I

Programmers have a desire to produce that one unique program which will establish for themselves a lasting reputation in the field. They do this by shortening the code, running the program faster, and using fewer variables. The result is more often a tarnished image of the programmer because the benefits seldom outweigh the costs incurred. Resist this temptation: a good programmer writes code that is simple to read and focuses on the problem to be solved.

To avoid surprises for the reader, a programmer must be conscious that part of his job is to map real-world entities (e.g., prices, temperatures, dollars, dates, and people's names) into the constructs of the Pascal language (e.g., numbers and strings). A programmer must not only choose a particular representation for an entity but must make sure that an operation validly represented in Pascal has meaning when applied to the original entity. For example, you can perform all arithmetic operations on numeric data. But while you can subtract two dollar amounts to get another dollar amount, it does not make sense to multiply two dollar amounts or to take the square root of a dollar amount.

More generally (see Figure 22), the input to any program represents some class of real-world entities: chess squares, wages, row numbers, cards, colors, and the like. A computation is required to transform these entities into other entities; for example, a chess move, an amount of money, a new row number, a card played, another color, and the like. The computer, however, can operate only in limited ways and on a limited set of entities like strings or integers. Thus, it is necessary to transform the real-world set of entities and operations into a program containing computer entities and operations. We shall say that a program is "straightforward" if each step in the computer algorithm has a simple correspondence to a step in a real-world algorithm that a person would use to solve the problem.

Straightforwardness and naturalness are closely connected to the clarity and readability of programs. Any programmer soon learns that understanding another programmer's code is

---

Figure 22. *Model for a typical programming task*

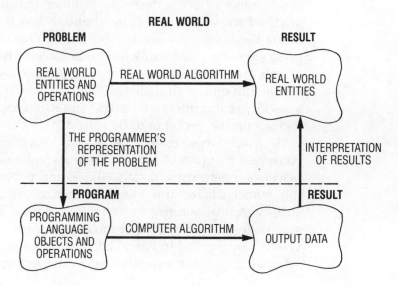

the anathema of the profession. Often programs do not accurately reflect the real-world algorithm corresponding to the numerical, array, logical, or string operations that are required for their computer implementation.

Try looking at any program that you wrote a month ago without peeking at the comments or the documentation. See if you immediately understand all of its details. Now imagine what it would be like for someone else who hadn't seen the program before. Clarity is a godsend to anyone who has to document, debug, extend, use, grade, or otherwise handle a computer program. Unless a program printout is being used by only one person, clarity is a double godsend to anyone having to use the program other than the original programmer.

Figure 23. *Two card-counting algorithms to find the rank of a missing card*

(a) Tricky card count

```
const
    NUMSUITS = 4;
    NUMRANKS = 13;
    NUMCARDS = 51;
    DECKSIZE = 52;
type
    CARDINFO = record
                    SUITVAL: 1..NUMSUITS;
                    RANKVAL: 1..NUMRANKS
               end;
    RANKNAME = packed array [1..5] of CHAR;
    DECKCONTENTS = array [1..DECKSIZE] of CARDINFO;
var
    I, RANK, COUNT: INTEGER;
    NAME:           RANKNAME;
    DECK:           DECKCONTENTS;

begin
    COUNT := 0;
    for I := 1 to NUMCARDS do begin
        RANK := DECK[I].RANKVAL;
        COUNT := (COUNT + RANK) mod NUMRANKS
    end;
    NAME := GETRANKNAME(NUMRANKS - COUNT);
    WRITELN ('Missing rank is: ', NAME)
end;
```

(b) Natural card count

```
const
    NUMSUITS = 4;
    NUMRANKS = 13;
    NUMCARDS = 51;
    DECKSIZE = 52;
type
    CARDINFO = record
                    SUITVAL: 1..NUMSUITS;
                    RANKVAL: 1..NUMRANKS
               end;
    RANKNAME     = packed array [1..5] of CHAR;
    RANKTALLY    = array [1..NUMRANKS] of INTEGER;
    DECKCONTENTS = array [1..DECKSIZE] of CARDINFO;
var
    COUNT:    RANKTALLY;
    I, RANK:  INTEGER;
    DECK:     DECKCONTENTS;
    NAME:     RANKNAME;

begin
    for RANK := 1 to NUMRANKS do
       COUNT[RANK] := 0;
    for I := 1 to NUMCARDS do begin
       RANK := DECK[I].RANKVAL;
       COUNT[RANK] := COUNT[RANK] + 1
    end;

    for RANK := 1 to NUMRANKS do
       if COUNT[RANK] < NUMSUITS then
          NAME := GETRANKNAME(RANK);
    WRITELN ('Missing rank is: ', NAME)
end;
```

For example, consider the following problem. Given a deck of 51 cards, we are asked to find the rank of the missing card (by computer, of course!). The deck is stored in a 51-element array called DECK. To make things simple, a function GETRANKNAME is assumed to be defined. GETRANKNAME takes the rank of a card (1 to 13) as its argument and maps the rank into a 5-character string:

"ACE " for 1,
"TWO " for 2,
. . .
"KING " for 13

Example 23 depicts two pieces of code, both of which claim to do the job correctly. Your problem is to discover *why* each one gives the correct result.

Figure 23(b) is obviously correct. In the real world, it corresponds to keeping a checklist of each rank and checking off the card ranks, one by one, until the deck is exhausted. Then the checklist is scanned to find out which card has been checked fewer than four times, and the selected rank is printed.

Figure 23(a) is also correct but far less straightforward. It has almost no correspondence to typical card table operations. It runs through the deck keeping a modulo 13 count of all the ranks. Afterwards it subtracts this count from 13 to get the rank of the missing card. If you are not convinced, try it.

Another area where natural programs have an advantage is that of *extendability*. Because a natural algorithm is analogous to real-world operations, extensions using these operations can often be made easily. Since a tricky algorithm usually depends on specific properties of numbers or strings, it usually cannot be applied to cases other than the original problem.

The program of Figure 23 illustrates this point well. Say that we now wish to extend the given programs to find the ranks of missing cards from a deck containing fewer than 51 cards. The algorithm of Figure 23(b) can be extended quite readily, as shown in Figure 24. In the corresponding real world, the sweep of the checklist is the same as before except that when we find that a card is missing, we print it, and see if any others are missing.

Figure 24.   *Extension of the natural card count*

```
const
    NUMSUITS = 4;
    NUMRANKS = 13;
    DECKSIZE = 52;
type
    CARDINFO = record
                    SUITVAL: 1..NUMSUITS;
                    RANKVAL: 1..NUMRANKS
               end;
    RANKNAME     = packed array [1..5] of CHAR;
    RANKTALLY    = array [1..NUMRANKS] of INTEGER;
    DECKCONTENTS = array [1..DECKSIZE] of CARDINFO;
var
    COUNT:    RANKTALLY;
    I, RANK:  INTEGER;
    DECK:     DECKCONTENTS;
    NAME:     RANKNAME;
    NUMMISSING: 1..DECKSIZE;

begin
    for RANK := 1 to NUMRANKS do
       COUNT[RANK] := 0;

    READLN (NUMCARDS);
    for I := 1 to NUMCARDS do begin
      RANK := DECK[I].RANKVAL;
      COUNT[RANK] := COUNT[RANK] + 1
    end;

    for RANK := 1 to NUMRANKS do
       if COUNT[RANK] < NUMSUITS then begin
          NAME := GETRANKNAME(RANK);
          NUMMISSING := NUMSUITS - COUNT[RANK];
          WRITELN (' There are ', NUMMISSING, ' with rank: ', NAME)
       end;
end;
```

Figure 23(a) *cannot* be extended, even to cover the case of two missing cards. The validity of the algorithm is based on the condition that there is only one missing card. With only one missing card, the difference between 13 and the count must be the rank of the missing card. With two or more missing cards, the sum of the ranks of the missing cards may be split in an arbitrary number of ways. In short, this algorithm fails because it is based on the particular properties of numbers instead of the properties of cards.

Before concluding the discussion of this proverb, remember that when you depart from a clear analogy with the problem, structure and clarity are frequently lost. Merging two or more modules of code in order to wring out those "extra lines" or adding a few lines in order to gain efficiency are both easy ways to prevent anyone from following the program. Considering the extra time needed to develop the special wrinkle and the extra testing time needed to check the new and often subtle boundary conditions, are you sure that fewer machine instructions or faster machine execution is likely?

There are cases where unusual methods are, in fact, justified, for example, to provide demanded efficiency of execution or economy of storage. However, before you resort to tricky programming, you should have a clear reason for doing so. Moreover, you should estimate the actual gain such programming will yield. Otherwise, you should stick to operations and objects that have a natural analogy in the real world.

Proverb 19   *YOUR OUTPUT IS NOT ONLY FOR YOU*

"He has gained every point who has mixed practicality with pleasure, by delighting the reader at the same time as instructing him."
HORACE Epistles, I

The best programmers that I have known have a bit of the poet in them: their output sings a little, rhymes a little. This quality often goes undetected by those who read the program later, who do not care how much time the programmer has spent in designing and debugging a program. The programmer who gets locked into a pattern of writing programs thinking only about results—the product that most people look for—generally produces output that pleases only the author and not the reader. Although the programmer knows what his program means and how to interpret the results, the same cannot be said for those who must wrestle with his product six months later.

This is such an obvious proverb. With all the work and effort required to write a program, i.e., to solve a problem, why should the output of a complex challenge simply look like a slipshod effort because it is poorly spaced, messy, or skimpy? Look at Figure 25(a). The output of this simple program is almost incomprehensible without an exact knowledge of the problem definition or of the program itself. The output of Figure 25(b), on the other hand, can be clearly understood by even the fledgling programmer.

The most pleasing poems and the most striking works of art have an organizing simplicity about them. They delight the reader and viewer as they instruct him. The moral of this proverb is that your output must be annotated so that it will stand on its own, not just for you but, if your effort is truly worthwhile, for all the future readers who will appreciate it.

Figure 25.   *Use of informative output*

(a) Poor

```
program REPORT (INPUT, OUTPUT);
    const
        NUMWEEKS = 4;
    type
        SALES = array [1..NUMWEEKS] of INTEGER;
    var
        WEEKLYSALES: SALES;
        SALESMAN, AVERAGESALE: INTEGER;
        NUMSALES, I: INTEGER;

function TOTALSALES (WEEKLYSALES: SALES): INTEGER;
    var
        I, TOTAL: INTEGER;
begin
    TOTAL := 0;
    for I := 1 to NUMWEEKS do
        TOTAL := TOTAL + WEEKLYSALES[I];
    TOTALSALES := TOTAL
end;
```

```
begin
   READ (SALESMAN);
   for I := 1 to NUMWEEKS do
      READ (WEEKLYSALES[I]);
   READLN;

   AVERAGESALE := TOTALSALES(WEEKLYSALES) div NUMWEEKS;

   WRITELN (SALESMAN, AVERAGESALE);
   for I := 1 to NUMWEEKS do
      WRITELN (WEEKLYSALES[I])
end.
```

```
-- Output from Figure 25(a)

   4  1000
1030
 980
1000
 990
```

(b) Better

```
program REPORT (INPUT, OUTPUT);
   const
      NUMWEEKS = 4;
   type
      SALES = array [1..NUMWEEKS] of INTEGER;
   var
      WEEKLYSALES:           SALES;
      SALESMAN, AVERAGESALE: INTEGER;
      NUMSALES, I:           INTEGER;

function TOTALSALES (WEEKLYSALES: SALES): INTEGER;
   var
      I, TOTAL: INTEGER;
begin
   TOTAL := 0;
   for I := 1 to NUMWEEKS do
      TOTAL := TOTAL + WEEKLYSALES[I];
   TOTALSALES := TOTAL
end;
```

```
begin
   WRITE ('Enter salesman id number: ');
   READLN (SALESMAN);
   WRITE ('Enter each weekly sales amount: ');
   for I := 1 to NUMWEEKS do
      READ (WEEKLYSALES[I]);

   WRITELN ('Salesman ', SALESMAN:1, ' sold:');
   for I := 1 to NUMWEEKS do
      WRITELN ('   $', WEEKLYSALES[I]:5, ' in week ', I:1);

   AVERAGESALE := TOTALSALES(WEEKLYSALES) div NUMWEEKS;

   WRITELN;
   WRITELN ('Average weekly sales:   $', AVERAGESALE:1)
end.


-- Output from Figure 25(b)

Salesman 4 Sold:
   $ 1030 in week 1
   $  980 in week 2
   $ 1000 in week 3
   $  990 in week 4

Average weekly sales:  $1000
```

Proverb 20   *REVIEW, REVIEW, REVIEW*

"When I get an ancient edition, I have it copied; after it is copied, I have it checked; after checking, have it set up, after setup, have it checked again; after checking, have it printed; after printing, have it checked again. Even with such care, there are two or three percent typographical errors. In this matter, where the eyes face something directly and closely, there are mistakes."

CHEN CHIJU (1558—1639), Yentse Yushih

The plight of this early Chinese writer is much the same as ours—and we have to solve our problems much the way he did, by reviewing again and again or, in our terms, by simply "hand-checking" the program. It is not easy to convince programmers that a program should be hand-checked before it is run. Yet run-time errors are the hardest to detect, and even if the system provides excellent debugging facilities, using the computer alone for this necessary review can be hazardous. The programmer may well be surprised at discovering errors like incorrect signs, infinite loops, and unusual conditions that lead to program crashes. More important, the benefit is that the programmer is likely to improve the program when it is seen in its "final" form.

The technique is simple. Choose a sample input, then calculate the output as if you were the computer, assuming nothing and using *exactly* what is written. See that each logical unit performs correctly and that the control sequence through the units is correct. If the program is too long or too complex to check in its entirety, then check each major section first, and later check the smaller units, assuming that the major units are correct. When choosing sample input, take special care to include the boundary conditions and other unusual cases. Failure to account for them is one of the most common programming errors.

For example, suppose you are writing a program that takes two non-negative integers as input, a dividend and a divisor, and prints out two numbers—the integer part of the quotient and the integer remainder.

Assume that Pascal does not have an integer division operator. That is, given the integer variables DIVIDEND, DIVISOR, QUOTIENT, and REMAINDER, assume that you cannot just say:

```
QUOTIENT    := DIVIDEND div DIVISOR;
REMAINDER   := DIVIDEND mod DIVISOR;
```

As a first pass, consider the program segment in Figure 26(a). Does this work? No. Why not? Checking by hand, we find that the program bombs out in the while statement. REMAINDER is initially undefined. (Remember, never assume that the computer assumes anything.) So we change the program as shown in Figure 26(b).

Does the program work now? Obviously not. Checking the boundary conditions by hand, we find that when the divisor is zero, the algorithm doesn't terminate. Since division by zero is undefined, we should process this case separately. It wouldn't be wise to leave the program in an infinite loop if we only considered the cost of computer time. So we change the program as shown in Figure 26(c).

It still doesn't work. Checking another boundary condition, we find that if the divisor exactly divides the dividend, we always get a quotient of 1 less than the correct value. For example, 10 divided by 5 is always 2 with a remainder of 0 not 1 with a remainder of 5. Correcting this error is easy, as shown in Figure 26(d).

Now this version works. Although the first error probably would have been picked up easily at run time, the other two probably would not. Their effects are input-dependent. Can you imagine searching for a data-dependent error in a long program that goes bad only once in a while?

Hand-check your program before running it, especially for the boundary conditions. We should like to think that with all the years of learning, like our Chinese friend, we can reduce the errors to two or three percent and perhaps, with the help of a code reader, to zero.

Figure 26.   *Hand-checking a program*

(a) First attempt

```
program DIVIDE (INPUT, OUTPUT);
    var
        DIVIDEND, DIVISOR, QUOTIENT, REMAINDER: INTEGER;

begin
    WRITE ('Enter dividend and divisor: ');
    READLN (DIVIDEND, DIVISOR);

    QUOTIENT := 0;
    while (REMAINDER > DIVISOR) do begin
        REMAINDER := REMAINDER - DIVISOR;
        QUOTIENT  := QUOTIENT + 1
    end;
    WRITELN ('Quotient = ', QUOTIENT:1, '   Remainder = ', REMAINDER:1)
end.
```

(b) Second attempt

```
program DIVIDE (INPUT, OUTPUT);
   var
      DIVIDEND, DIVISOR, QUOTIENT, REMAINDER: INTEGER;

begin
   WRITE ('Enter dividend and divisor: ');
   READLN (DIVIDEND, DIVISOR);

   QUOTIENT  := 0;
   REMAINDER := DIVIDEND;
   while (REMAINDER > DIVISOR) do begin
      REMAINDER := REMAINDER - DIVISOR;
      QUOTIENT  := QUOTIENT + 1
   end;
   WRITELN ('Quotient = ', QUOTIENT:1, ' Remainder = ', REMAINDER:1)
end.
```

(c) Third attempt

```
program DIVIDE (INPUT, OUTPUT);
   var
      DIVIDEND, DIVISOR, QUOTIENT, REMAINDER: INTEGER;

begin
   WRITE ('Enter dividend and divisor: ');
   READLN (DIVIDEND, DIVISOR);

   if DIVISOR = 0 then
      WRITELN ('Attempt to divide by 0.')
   else
      begin
         QUOTIENT := 0;
         REMAINDER := DIVIDEND;
         while (REMAINDER > DIVISOR) do begin
            QUOTIENT  := QUOTIENT + 1;
            REMAINDER := REMAINDER - DIVISOR
         end;
         WRITELN ('Quotient = ', QUOTIENT:1, '  Remainder = ', REMAINDER:1)
      end
end.
```

(d) Fourth attempt

```
program DIVIDE (INPUT, OUTPUT);
   var
      DIVIDEND, DIVISOR, QUOTIENT, REMAINDER: INTEGER;

begin
   WRITE ('Enter divident and divisor: ');
   READLN (DIVIDEND, DIVISOR);

   if DIVISOR = 0 then
      WRITELN ('Attempt to divide by 0.')
   else
      begin
         QUOTIENT  := 0;
         REMAINDER := DIVIDEND;
         while (REMAINDER >= DIVISOR) do begin
            QUOTIENT  := QUOTIENT + 1;
            REMAINDER := REMAINDER - DIVISOR
         end;
         WRITELN ('Quotient = ', QUOTIENT:1, ' Remainder = ', REMAINDER:1)
      end
end.
```

Proverb 21	*CAREFUL PROGRAMMERS DON'T HAVE ACCIDENTS*	*"what in hell have i done to deserve all these kittens."* DON MARQUIS *mehetibel and her kittens*

The top-down approach to programming is the answer to the question: "What the hell have I done?"—a question that may not need to be asked at all if the approach is followed conscientiously. The top-down approach is not only an effective tool in program development, but it is just as valuable in program verification. This simply means that the main program and upper levels are verified first and the most primitive modules last.

Top-down testing is a strategy which says:

** Test a given module *before* testing any modules that it calls.

Verifying from the top down should be obvious, especially if a program is being written top-down. Programs of this type are usually well modularized, and it is unwise to verify lower levels if the upper levels may be incorrect. Since the sections of the program are integral units that can stand on their own, the most important ones should be verified first. A schematic illustration of a program is shown in Figure 27. Encircled sections indicate that the set of enclosed modules is to be considered as a unit. The program has five main modules, each of which can be verified separately. The verification process starts with the main program. As an upper module is verified, the process continues through lower levels until the entire program has been verified. Verifying the entire program in one lump is to be avoided.

Consider Figure 28, a program for summing the first N positive integers for differing values of N. Clearly, the answers generated by the program are incorrect. The programmer decides to check the main program loop and adds the verification lines shown, which print out the inner loop control variable and the current value of the sum. When the revised program is run, we can easily see that on iteration 1 for the second value of N, the sum is already 22; that is, SUM is not properly initialized. Moving the SUM initialization statement to just before the inner for loop solves the problem.

One popular verification aid available in several implementations is the "trace." Basically, a trace is a facility which will monitor the behavior of prespecified variables or functions. The trace of a variable can monitor any use or change of its value. The trace of a function can monitor each call, its arguments, and its returned value. The programmer can use a trace to verify that functions are being called with proper arguments and correct returned values. In function-oriented programs or programs using recursion, traces can be invaluable. One word of caution: overuse of the trace feature has been known to produce voluminous output with no useful information.

Systems that implement Pascal ordinarily offer other verification facilities. Does your system support any program design, development, or documentation aids? Does your system support a cross-reference lister, program librarian, test data

Figure 27.   *Picture of a program designed top-down*

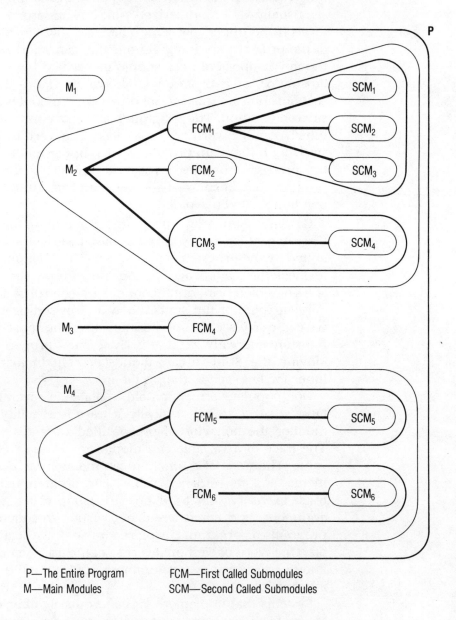

P—The Entire Program   FCM—First Called Submodules
M—Main Modules   SCM—Second Called Submodules

generator, test supervisor, module testing, execution monitor, or output analyzer package? Be sure to find out what features your system provides, and incorporate them into programs you write. If you are lucky enough to be using Pascal for the Macintosh or Instant Pascal for the Apple II, some terrific runtime aids come with the system. Although it may not be wise to use implementation-dependent features as part of a final program, it would be foolish not to utilize them for verification.

There is no doubt that you will ask yourself "What the hell have I done?" many times in program verification. But if you make the best use of the verification facilities in your computer system, you will know what you have done. One who expects the worst is doubly blessed: even when the worst happens, you will be prepared; if the best is your lot, you will be quietly proud that neither result was an accident.

Figure 28.   ***Use of the writeln statement for verification***

```
program SUM (INPUT, OUTPUT);

{ -- Program to sum the first N positive integers. }

    var
        SUM, I, J, N: INTEGER;
        NUMSEQUENCES: INTEGER;

begin
    SUM := 0;
    WRITE ('Enter number of sequences: ');
    READLN (NUMSEQUENCES);

    for I := 1 to NUMSEQUENCES do begin
        WRITE ('Enter number of terms: ');
        READLN (N);
        for J := 1 to N do
            SUM := SUM + J;
        WRITELN ('Sum of first ', N:1, ' integers is ', SUM:1)
    end
end.
```

```
-- Output from Figure 28

Sum of first 6 integers is 21
Sum of first 3 integers is 27

-- Verification Line Inserted Before Writeln Statement:

WRITELN ('Iteration ', J:1,  '  Sum ', SUM:2);


-- Output from Figure 28 with Verification Line

Iteration 1  Sum  1
Iteration 2  Sum  3
Iteration 3  Sum  6
Iteration 4  Sum 10
Iteration 5  Sum 15
Iteration 6  Sum 21
Sum of first 6  integers is 21
Iteration 1  Sum 22
Iteration 2  Sum 24
Iteration 3  Sum 27
Sum of first 3  integers is 27
```

4 *AND OF COURSE . . .*

❧

*"LET US HEAR THE CONCLUSION OF
THE WHOLE MATTER."*

Ecclesiastes 12:13

Proverb 22 | *HAVE SOMEONE ELSE READ THE WORK* | *"An old man has crossed more bridges than a young man has crossed streets."*
Chinese proverb

The sequence of these proverbs is a matter of choice, but if there is one "proverb among proverbs" for programmers, it should be this one. Few programmers can, or should, enjoy any kind of "poetic licence" in their work—the parameters of the discipline demand that one's effort be open for inspection and criticism. In fact, this proverb should be understood as a requirement of good practice as much as any proverb that has gone before.

Having someone else read the work does *not* mean just having someone else read the final code. Even a developing definition should be read by someone else, as well as the program specifications, the levels of the top-down design, and the test plans.

The benefits of a second reading are legion: identifying unwarranted assumptions, unintentional omissions, unnecessary complexities, or just plain mistakes. But more important, both you and your reader will improve your problem-solving and programming techniques by this kind of mutual involvement. This is the principle of programming teams that is so important in fostering cooperative communication, maintaining team standards, promoting quality documentation, and generally keeping abreast of the total work effort.

Consider Figure 29, which contains two simple errors—both easy to make and both difficult to detect. The programmer who wrote the code would find the errors almost impossible to detect by rereading the code even one more time. Try to find them yourself.

Here are a few suggestions to make your work-reading more effective:

1. *Make sure you have a piece of work in writing.*

2. *Don't give someone else 20 pages at a time; 3 or 4 will do.*

3. *Focus on the work itself, not on the persons or personalities that produced it.*

4. *Do it on a regular basis: put it in your plan.*

5. *Don't confuse work-reading with a "meeting"— it is not a structural function, it is a good programming habit.*

6. *Take special care in looking for missing details, fuzzy statements, and boundary conditions.*

If the piece of work is too long or too complex to check in its entirety, check each major section first—or better, just remember the last proverb.

Work-reading requires extra time and demands extra care, but it is a small price to pay for the benefits listed above. At first, the practice may seem time-consuming, annoying, and even embarrassing at times. But given time, abiding with this proverb will have a marked impact on your work. You should practice as a reader for others, too. You will find, as I have, that *all aspects of good programming practice are improved by work-reading.* In no time at all, you will be crossing more bridges than streets—and you don't have to be an old man to do it.

Figure 29.   ***The compiler catches one error, but who catches the other?***

```
program ROOTS (INPUT, OUTPUT);

{ -- Program to find the real roots of the equation:
  --     A*(X*X) + (B*X) + C = 0  }

var
   A, B, C,
   X1, X2,
   DISCRIMINANT: REAL;

begin
   WRITE ('Enter A, B, and C: ');
   READLN (A, B, C);

   if A = 0.0 then
      if B = 0.0 then
         WRITELN ('This is the degenerate case')
      else
         begin
            X := -C / B;
            WRITELN ('One real root. . . X = ', X)
         end;

   if (A <> 0.0) and (B <> 0.0) then begin
      DISCRIMINANT := (B*B) - (4*A*C);

      if DISCRIMINANT < 0.0 then
         WRITELN ('No real roots')
      else if DISCRIMINANT = 0.0 then
         begin
            X1 := -B / 2*A;
            X2 := X1;
            WRITELN ('Equal real roots: X1 = ', X1, ' X2 = ', X2)
         end
      else if DISCRIMINANT > 0.0 then
         begin
            X1 := (-B + SQRT(DISCRIMINANT)) / 2*A;
            X2 := (-B - SQRT(DISCRIMINANT)) / 2*A;
            WRITELN ('Distinct real roots: X1 = ', X1, ' X2 = ', X2)
         end
   end
end.
```

Proverb 23   *WHAT HAVE YOU READ LATELY?*

"No book is worth anything until it is worth much; nor is it serviceable until it has been read, and re-read, and loved, and loved again; and marked, so that you can refer to the passages you want in it."
JOHN RUSKIN   Sesame and Lilies, Of Kings' Treasuries, Sect. 32

A friend of a friend was taking a year off and was asked, in an offhanded manner, what was he looking forward to the most? He said, "Oh, of course, to read! Teaching does not give one the chance to read. I'm always afraid I may have missed something."

This is what this proverb is all about—reading. There are two facets to reading:

1. *Technical: the reading associated with your system— language reference manuals, system manuals, utilities manuals, operating and environment guides;*

2. *Literary: the reading associated with your field—magazines, journals, and books.*

The objectives are:

1. *To become a master of the system;*

2. *To develop better perspectives.*

The common failures are:

1. *Clinging to a timid subset of a system;*

2. *Becoming a "hacker" of the trade.*

Nothing can be as boring as system manuals. Why go back to read them again? Because somewhere in all those poorly written manuals, the same kind that you are dedicated to improve, there is a kernel of knowledge that you may have overlooked. After programming for a while, we tend to settle into our own kind of convenient language for our host computer. Periodically rereading the manuals helps to remind us that there are many useful features that, even though we don't use them every day, may be just the ones we need at a later date.

For example: do you know how Pascal deals with character strings? Do you know how integer division works? Do you know all the predefined mathematical functions and the file manipulation capabilities? Does your implementation allow reference to externally compiled procedures? How about the number of significant figures kept by your particular machine? How is the program header defined on your implementation? Can input or output files be structured or segmented? What are the default specifications for output of standard data types? How are carriage control characters defined?

As you survey the literature, you will encounter the writings of programmers of many stripes: hackers, boring, introverted, machine-like, uncultured, and so on. These impressions need not be true as you read more deeply into their writings. Programmers who publish do so to advance their profession because they understand that their experience is as beneficial to their peers as the writings of their mentors was to them. While there is no substitute for project experience, our own skills will be improved by reading. Consider:

1. *an article on professional ethics;*

2. *an experiment on the philosophies of command languages;*

3. *a report on a new printer;*

4. *a book on software engineering;*

5. *data on which features of System X are little used;*

6. *a report on Pascal's successor: Modula-2;*

7. *a curriculum for computer science;*

8. *a product review.*

These can be worth reading, even when they may be only marginal to your current project.

The question is: what is the state of the art? As you make your contribution, you must read to see what other contributions are being made. Rereading your own manuals and the current literature goes with the territory. You may be pleased at what you find.

Proverb 24   *DON'T BE AFRAID TO START OVER*

"To dry one's eyes and laugh at a fall, and baffled, get up and begin again."
ROBERT BROWNING   Life in a Love, Stanza 2

Odd as it may seem, the first and last of these proverbs are encouraging! Don't panic and don't be afraid to start over! I say this because I hope that you should never have to lean on either proverb—all the ones that come between should be enough support.

Sometimes during program development, testing, or modification, it may seem that the program you are working on is becoming unusually cumbersome. So many user-requirements changes may have been thrown at you that the problem itself is different from the original proposal. Other than the first and last, maybe none of these proverbs seemed to apply in developing the program and the result is that the program produces error after error.

No matter. At some point, pruning and restoring a blighted tree is an impossible task—better to replace it with a seedling. The same is true of blighted computer programs. Restoring a structure that has been so distorted by patches and deletions or trying to find a program with a seriously weak algorithm simply isn't worth the time. The best that can result is a long, inefficient, unintelligible program that defies even more maintenance.

You have to develop a heartless sense of recognizing that when the program is hopelessly in trouble, chuck it out and start over again. And don't let your ego stand in the way. The lessons that you learned on the old program can be applied to the new one and yield the desired result in far less time with far less trouble.

Use these two proverbs to advantage. Don't panic, and start over. Above all, don't try to convert a bad program into a good one—bring out a new model.

EXERCISES FOR PART I

Exercise 1   *Problem Definitions*

Consider the following program specification:

"Write a program that computes the weight in kilograms of a weight expressed in pounds and ounces."

Upon careful thought, the above specification reveals many points that would be unclear to a programmer. Rewrite the above specification so that *any* two programs written to solve the problem would have *exactly* the same input-output characteristics, for example, the same input format, the same number of significant digits, the same headings, and so forth. (Note: You are to write a program specification, *not* a program; a good definition may require a full page.)

Exercise 2   *Problem Definitions*

Each of the following program specifications is either missing one or more critical definitions or is unclear, misleading, or confusing. (a) How are the program specifications deficient? (b) Rewrite all or part of one program specification to make it as clear and explicit as possible, that is, so that there can be no doubt as to what the program should do. (c) In general, what does *any* program specification require to make it as clear and explicit as possible?

Program specification 1   Given the following rates of payment, write a program that will compute the monthly commission for a car salesman.

Grade of Salesman	Commission Rate
1	$5.00 + 0.50% for first ten sales $7.50 + 0.75% every subsequent sale
2	$7.50 + 0.75% for first ten sales $10.00 + 1.00% every subsequent sale
3	$10.00 + 1.00% for first ten sales $12.50 + 1.25% every subsequent sale

4	$12.50 + 1.25% for first ten sales
	$15.00 + 1.50% every subsequent sale
5	$15.00 + 1.50% for first ten sales
	$17.50 + 1.75% every subsequent sale

The input should be the grade of the salesman and the number of sales he has made for the month. The output should read "THE SALESMAN'S COMMISSION IS $ C," where c is the salesman's commission.

Program specification 2   The Programmer's Equity Life Insurance Company offers policies of $25,000, $50,000, and $100,000. The cost of a policyholder's annual premium is determined as follows. There is a basic fee that depends upon the amount of coverage carried. This is $25 for a $25,000 policy, $50 for a $50,000 policy, and $100 for a $100,000 policy.

In addition to the basic fee, there are two additional charges depending on the age and lifestyle of the policyholder. The first additional charge is determined by multiplying this by either 1½, 2, or 3 if the policy is at the $25,000, $50,000, or $100,000 level, respectively. The second additional charge is determined by the policyholder's lifestyle, which is a rating of the danger of harm resulting from his occupation and hobbies. This rating is determined by company experts from a questionnaire returned by the policy applicant. They return a rating from 1 to 5 in steps of 1, with 1 being the safest rating. The charge is then determined by multiplying this rating by 5 and then further multiplying by 1½, 2, or 3 if the policy is either at the $25,000, $50,000, or $100,000 level, respectively. The total premium is found by adding together these separately determined charges.

Write a program to output tables of yearly premium costs for men of ages from 21 to 75 for all amounts of policy value and safety ratings.

Exercise 3   *Problem Definitions*

Upon very careful reading, the problem definition of Figure 4 shows several deficiencies. The *exact* input-output characteristics are not really fully specified. Describe these deficiencies.

Exercise 4	*Functions and Procedures*

Consider a program with the following specification:

Input: a positive integer N
Output: the values SUM(N), $SUM^2(N)$, $SUM^3(N)$, and
         $SUM^4(N)$

where SUM(N) denotes the sum of the first N integers, $SUM^2(N)$ denotes SUM(SUM(N)), and so forth.

1. *Write the program* without *the use of functions or subroutines.*

2. *Write the program using functions or procedures.*

The differences can be quite striking.

Exercise 5	*Goto's*

Restructure the sequence of the following statements to eliminate all goto's and statement numbers; make the sequence as *short* and clear as possible. (Note: Can it be done with only two assignment statements?)

```
begin
    goto 3;
1:  if X = 0 then
        goto 9
    else
        goto 5;

5:  if X > MAXVALUE then
        goto 6
    else
        goto 4;

9:  WRITELN (X);
    goto 7;

3:  READLN (X);
    goto 1;
```

```
6: X := SQRT(X);

8: X := X*X + X;
   goto 9;

4: X := X*X;
   goto 8;

7: {do nothing}
end;
```

Exercise 6 **Goto's**

Consider the conventional 8 by 8 array representation of a chessboard whose squares are denoted by (1,1), (1,2), . . . , (8,8) and the problem of placing eight queens on the board so that *no* queen can capture *any other* queen. In chess, a queen can capture another piece if the queen lies on the same row, column, or diagonal as the other piece.

1. *Write a program to read in the coordinates of eight queens and print "TRUE" if no queen can capture any other and "FALSE" otherwise.*

2. *Draw a flow diagram for the program.*

3. *Score the program according to the following rule:*
    SCORE = 100—10*(number-of-crossing-lines)

Exercise 7 **Syntax**

It is important that a programmer be able to detect simple syntactic errors. Consider the following program to compute PI using the series, $PI^4/96 = 1/1^4 + 1/3^4 + 1/5^4 + \ldots$. How many syntactic errors are there? Correct the program so that there are no errors.

```
    N := 0;
    while (ABS(TEMP) < EPSILON) do
        begin
            N := N + 1
            TEMP := 1 / (2N - 1)**4;
            SUB  := SUM + TEMP
        end;
    PI := SQRT(SQRT(DELTA*SUM));
```

Exercise 8   *Syntax*

Which of the following examples are syntactically correct instances of the given Pascal categories? Correct the erroneous examples. If possible, you should assume *any* suitable specification statements needed to make a construct correct. That is, the question is "Is there any conceivable program where the construct could be correct?"

1. *Arithmetic Expression*
   ```
   F(F)
   ```

2. *Arithmetic Expression*
   ```
   P[Q] + X**X**X - 1/2
   ```

3. *If Statement*
   ```
   if (X and Y > 4) then
       WRITELN (X)
   ```

4. *For Statement*
   ```
   for I = 1 to N do
       X[I] := X[I] + X[I]
   ```

5. *Type Declaration*

   ```
   type
       BOOLEAN := (TRUE, FALSE);
   ```

6. *Case Statement*
   ```
   case COLOR of
       RED    := GREEN;
       GREEN  := 'GO';
       YELLOW := 'SLOW DOWN';
       RED    := 'STOP'
   end;
   ```

7. *Function*

```
function F(X, Y, Z): REAL;
    F := X * Y + Z
end;
```

8. *Function*

```
function F(X, Y, Z: REAL): REAL;
    var
        SUM: REAL;
    begin
    for I := 1 to Z do
        SUM := SUM + X[I] + Y[I];
    F := SUM
end;
```

9. *Assignment Statement*

```
I := F[I].B[I]
```

10. *Comparison*

```
type
    COLOR = (RED, WHITE, BLUE);
    ...

var
    C: COLOR;
    ...
    if C < RED then
    ...
```

Exercise 9   *Mnemonic Names*

The following statement sequence performs a well-known, simple arithmetic computation. By basically changing all identifiers, rewrite the program so that it clearly illuminates the intended computation.

```
program STRANGE (INPUT, OUTPUT);
const
    FOUR = 4.0E0;
    FIVE = 3.0E0;
    PLUS = 'PLUS';
var
    LEFT, RIGHT, MIDDLE, ALL,
    ONE, LEFT1, LEFT2, RIGHT1: REAL;
```

```
begin
   while not EOLN do begin
      WRITE ('Enter three values: ');
      READLN (LEFT, MIDDLE, RIGHT);
      RIGHT1 := LEFT*RIGHT*FOUR;
      LEFT1  := MIDDLE*MIDDLE - RIGHT1;
      LEFT2  := SQRT(LEFT1);
      ONE    := -(LEFT2 - MIDDLE)/(FIVE*LEFT);
      ALL    := -(LEFT2 + MIDDLE)/(2EO*LEFT);
      WRITELN (ONE, PLUS, ALL)
   end
end.
```

Exercise 10 *Change*

Consider a program to compute the gravitational force F exerted between two planets M1 and M2 located (over time) at different orbital distances from each other. In particular, let

$$M1 = \text{mass of planet } 1 = 6 * 10^{24}$$
$$M2 = \text{mass of planet } 2 = 8 * 10^{25}$$
$$G \ \ = \text{gravitational constant} = 6.7 * 10^{-11}$$
$$F \ \ = G * M1 * M2 / (R^2)$$

Write a program to output F for values of R varying from $100*10^8$ to $110*10^8$ in increments of $0.01*10^8$ such that all constants are specified in a data statement and *no* constant terms are recomputed.

Exercise 11 *Output*

The following input/output was generated by the use of a working program in a time-sharing environment:

```
Input:  What is N1 and N2?
        5, 10
Output: 5          25
        6          36
        7          49
        8          64
        9          81
       10         100
```

Rewrite the input/output so that the average "man on the street" would be able to understand what the input numbers 5 and 10 represent and what the output means.

Exercise 12 ## *Work-Reading*

Describe two more advantages to having someone else read the work you produce during the various phases of a programming project. Describe two disadvantages or bottlenecks.

Exercise 13 ## *Reading the Manuals*

Reread your Pascal manual and find three features that you had forgotten or did not know existed. For each feature, give an example of how it would be more useful.

Exercise 14 ## *Reading the Manuals*

Answer precisely the following questions with reference to your Pascal manual:

1. *What type names are predefined?*

2. *How many dimensions can an array have?*

3. *What is a legal subscript?*

4. *In what contexts can the logical values of TRUE and FALSE appear?*

5. *Are matrix commands available?*

6. *How many significant digits are kept for real numbers?*

Exercise 15   *Code Rewrite*

The following program performs a simple, well-known computation. Rewrite the program so that it clearly illuminates the intended computation. In the process, eliminate goto's, use mnemonic names, and produce good output.

```
program GOTOS (INPUT, OUTPUT);
    label
        1, 2, 3, 5;
    var
        A, B, C, D, F, G: REAL;

begin
    goto 1;

2: READLN (A);
   F := A * A;
   goto 3;

1: READLN (B);
   G := B * B;
   goto 2;

3: if (A <= 0) or (B <= 0)
       then
           goto 5
       else
           begin
               C := F + G;
               D := SQRT(C);
               WRITELN (D)
           end;

5: { exit }
end.
```

Exercise 16   *It Worked the First Time*

Write a program that determines whether an input string is a palindrome. A palindrome is a string that reads the same forward and backward. For example, LEVEL is a palindrome but

PALINDROME is not. When the program is running correctly, score it using the following formula:

```
SCORE = 100 - (5*times-resubmitted)
            - (2*number-of-lines-changed)
```

Exercise 17   *Intermediate Variables*

Usually a complex mathematical expression can be coded as a single arithmetic expression. However, for the sake of clarity it is often advantageous to split up a lengthy arithmetic expression and use intermediate variables. Give an example where clarity is gained with the use of intermediate variables. Give an example where the obvious result is program efficiency. Give an example where the use of inappropriate or excessive intermediate variables causes confusion.

Exercise 18   *Guess the Proverb*

The following program is supposed to have the following characteristics:

Input: a sequence of n nonzero integers terminated by the integer zero

Output: the MEAN (the sum of all values divided by n)

$$SUM(x) / n$$

and standard deviation,

$$SQRT(SUM(x^2) / n - MEAN^2)$$

of the integers in the input sequence.

```
program STATISTICS (INPUT, OUTPUT);
    var
        A, B, C  : INTEGER;
        D, E, F, G: REAL;
begin
    A := 0;  B := 0;  C := 0;  D := 0;
    D := 0;  E := 0;  F := 0;
```

```
      repeat
         while not EOLN do
            begin
               READLN (G);
               A := A + G;
               B := B + 1;
               C := C + SQR(G)
            end
      until G <= F;

      D := A/B;
      E := SQRT(C/B - SQR)A));
      I := F - D/F;
      WRITELN (E, E)
   end.
```

Of all the programming proverbs, which *single* proverb, if properly followed, would be most valuable in converting the above program to a good program? (Note: There really *is* a best answer.)

Exercise 19 *The Pascal Quiz*

A user who has a *very thorough* knowledge of any language should be able to detect erroneous programs that prematurely terminate because of a syntactic (compile-time) or semantic (run-time) error. In the absence of a formal definition of a language, the definition of constructs that produce fatal syntactic or semantic errors must ultimately be based on a particular implementation. To treat this issue precisely, consider the insertion of print statements as the first and last executable statements in a program, and let us adopt the following definitions:

1. *A program is "syntactically invalid" if the first print statement is not executed, that is, if the implementation finds an unacceptable error.*

2. *A program is "syntactically valid" if the first print statement is executed, that is, if the implementation detects no severe errors, translates the program into machine language, and begins execution.*

3. *A program is "semantically invalid" (but syntactically valid) if the first but not the last print statement is executed, that is, the program is started but not completed.*

4. *A program is "semantically valid" (and syntactically valid) if the first and last print statements are executed, that is, if the program is executed without abnormal termination.*

To test your knowledge of the above issues in Pascal, you are asked to answer two simple questions about the programs given in the Pascal quiz below.

Is the first WRITELN statement (which prints "START") executed?
Is the last WRITELN statement (which prints "FINISH") executed?

Check the appropriate spaces or put your answers on a separate sheet. Note: It is quite difficult to answer all questions correctly.

1. START: Yes ___ No ___
FINISH: Yes ___ No ___

```
program ONE (INPUT, OUTPUT);
    label 6;
    var
        A, B, C: INTEGER;

begin
    WRITELN ('Start');
    A := 1;

6: B := 2;
    goto 6;

6: C := 33;
    WRITELN ('Finish')
end.
```

2. START: Yes ____   No ____
    FINISH: Yes ____   No ____

```
program TWO (INPUT, OUTPUT);
   var
      X: REAL;

function P(function F(X: REAL): REAL): REAL;
begin
   P := F(1.4, 2.6, 1.9)
end;

begin
   WRITELN ('Start');
   X := P(MAX);
   WRITELN ('Finish')
end.
```

3. START: Yes ____   No ____
    FINISH: Yes ____   No ____

```
program THREE (INPUT, OUTPUT);
   var
      A: REAL;

procedure P(var X, Y: REAL);
begin
   X := X + 1;
   Y := Y*(X + 1)
end;

begin
   WRITELN ('Start');
   A := 2;
   P(A, 1);
   WRITELN ('Finish')
end.
```

4. START: Yes ____   No ____
    FINISH: Yes ____   No ____

```
program FOUR (INPUT, OUTPUT);
   var
      A: REAL;
```

```
procedure P(var X, Y: REAL);
begin
   X := X + 1;
   Y := Y*(X + 1)
end;

begin
   WRITELN ('Start');
   A := 2;
   P (A, TRUE);
   WRITELN ('Finish')
end.
```

5. START: Yes ___   No ___
FINISH: Yes ___   No ___

```
program FIVE (INPUT, OUTPUT);
   var
      J: INTEGER;

function G (function F(X: INTEGER): INTEGER; N: INTEGER): INTEGER;
   var
      N: INTEGER;
begin
   if N = 0 then
      G := 1
   else
      G := N*G(F, N-1)
end;

function FACT(N: INTEGER): INTEGER;
begin
   FACT := G(FACT, N)
end;

begin
   WRITELN ('Start');
   J := FACT(5);
   WRITELN ('Finish')
end.
```

6. START: Yes ____ No ____
   FINISH: Yes ____ No ____

```
program SIX (INPUT, OUTPUT);
    type
        BOOLEAN = INTEGER;
    var
        B: BOOLEAN;

begin
    WRITELN ('Start');
    B := 1;
    WRITELN ('Finish');
end.
```

PART
TWO

BEYOND THE
PROVERBS

PROGRAM STANDARDS

❧

*"WE COME FROM A WORLD WHERE WE
HAVE KNOWN INCREDIBLE STANDARDS OF
EXCELLENCE."*

*Thornton Wilder
The Bridge of San Luis Rey, Chapter 4*

The Pascal language has been with us for many years, yet the writing of high-quality Pascal programs has remained a matter of personal style. The thrust of this chapter is to go beyond the "proverbs" and present some rigorous standards for the writing of Pascal programs. Developing rigorous program standards is not easy, for the rules must be unambiguous. They must also be of sufficient merit that a programmer will not be unduly stifled by their adoption. We have followed this chapter's standards throughout this book.

The importance of developing such standards is clear. For managers, instructors, and programmers, there is a need to develop uniform rules so that everyone may more easily understand programs, a need to develop coding techniques that reduce the complexity of programs, and a need to control the entire software development effort.

I make no attempt here to encompass every feature of the Pascal language. No standard can cover every aspect of a given programming problem. Nevertheless, the standards presented here should go a long way to promote quality programs.

The general issue of programming standards is indeed complex. When the initial boundaries of a language are restricted, the programmer resistance can be great. In addition, any attempt to promote or enforce such a set of standards must resolve a number of difficult issues.

First, exceptional cases must be avoided when writing a standard. It is critical that the standard be as solid as possible, for otherwise, the credibility of the entire activity can be undermined. Possible exceptional cases must thus be carefully screened before the standard is adopted.

Second, there is the issue of enforcement. What mechanism should be set up to enforce the standards? Can the standards really be enforced without some kind of automatic aids? What about the professional programmer who does not see any reason for a particular standard or its use in a particular case? These questions are difficult to answer.

Third, given that some method of enforcement has been adopted and given that some useful exception does occur, how is the exception to be handled? While an ideal standard has no exceptions, when exceptions do arise, they have to be handled without undermining the credibility of the entire effort.

Fourth, there are a number of human factors that must be faced, especially when standards are being developed. For one, choices may be a matter of taste, and there are bound to be some arbitrary decisions. Further, there may be some initial overhead in following the standards. The human tendency is to get on with the job, i.e., code. This tendency must be resisted, for if the standards are correct, breaking the standards is shortsighted.

Finally, one must be very careful to avoid expecting too much from the standards, for eventually the problem-dependent features of a program will demand special attention. While the adoption of good standards may help in producing good solutions to the problem at hand, ultimately the style and expertise of the practicing programmer will become paramount.

GENERAL REQUIREMENTS

[Gen-1]   *Someone should be appointed to maintain and enforce the standards.*

The rationale here is to refine the standards, monitor them, and allow exceptions, but *only* in a controlled manner. It is critical that all programming standards, unless revoked, be followed to the very last detail. The method for enforcing the standards is left to the particular instructor, team leader, or manager.

[Gen-2]   *All full programs shall include header comments.*

For example:

```
{ -- ** Program Title:      Brief title
  -- ** Written By:         Name of author(s)
  -- ** Date Written:       Date
  --
  -- ** Program Summary:    Brief program summary
       . . .
  -- ** Input and Output Files:
  --        file-name:      Brief description of use
       . . .
```

The rationale here is to give a quick synopsis of the program's intent, input and output files, and title information, so that a program has some minimal internal documentation.

[Gen-3]   *For each application there should be an adopted set of standard user-defined names and abbreviations.*

The standard words should be chosen *before* coding. The following set of names is a very small sample of those that might be adopted for a Pascal application.

```
SYM           -- Abbreviation for SYMBOL
MSG           -- Abbreviation for MESSAGE
NUM           -- Abbreviation for NUMBER
POS           -- Abbreviation for POSITION

GETSYM        -- For a subroutine to input symbols
SYMLENGTH     -- For lengths of symbols
PUSH          -- For a subroutine to put symbols on a stack
POP           -- For a subroutine to remove symbols from a stack
STACK         -- For a stack of attributes
```

115

```
KEYVALUE        -- For an array of keyword values
DIGIT           -- For numeric characters
LETTER          -- For alphabetic characters
EOFMSG          -- For an end-of-file message
```

The rationale here is to develop a well-accepted set of naming conventions and to reduce the time spent by programmers in devising good mnemonic words. This standard is intended to promote program readability and to prevent confusion caused by having different names for the same entities.

[Gen-4]   *Comments that occupy a full line must begin with -- and be written in lowercase.*

The idea here is to make the comments visually separate from the program itself. Thus instead of something like

```
{ FIND NEXT ROOT. }
INTERVAL := EPSILON;
ESTIMATE := F(X2 - X1) / 2.0;
```

use

```
{ -- Find next root. }
INTERVAL := EPSILON;
ESTIMATE := F(X2 - X1) / 2.0;
```

The latter is easier on the reader.

[Gen-5]   *No program unit should exceed two pages in length.*

The rationale here is to force program units (i.e., main programs, functions, or subroutines) to be isolated on at most two pages of text. In general, each program unit should occupy no more than a single page of text. However, due to the frequent exceptional cases where initializations or repeated computations require extensive code, the standard allows program units to occupy up to two pages of text.

[Gen-6]   *Each procedure or function should begin on a new page, or (for short procedures and functions) with a break of at least four blank lines.*

If you have ever spent ten minutes trying to locate a procedure in a long listing, you will believe the wisdom of this rule.

[Gen-7]   *Each line should have fewer than 72 characters.*

This one sounds easy, but many programmers use wide printers that can take 120 characters per line. So, why not go beyond 72 characters? Because

1. *Long lines are difficult to read.*

2. *Huge indents happen too easily.*

3. *Most copiers use standard (8.5 by 11) paper.*

4. *Large pieces of paper are cumbersome for filing.*

And most important,

5. *There is simply no need to exceed 72 characters.*

It's silly to break this rule.

[Gen-8]   *Each statement must begin on a separate line.*

This means that

```
COUNT := 0; SUM := 0;
```

and

```
while NEXTCHAR <> BLANK do READ(NEXTCHAR);
```

are not allowed. The point is that such statements can be over-looked. Placing each on a new line, i.e.,

```
COUNT := 0;
SUM   := 0;
```

and

```
while NEXTCHAR <> BLANK do
READ (NEXTCHAR)
```

makes a simple rule that the reader can depend on. Note: Pro-grammers who are in a hurry often break this rule.

DECLARATIONS

[Dcl-1]   ***All scalars (numbers and characters) that remain constant throughout a program must be specified in a constant declaration.***

The rationale here is to isolate constants and, if need be, to allow changes without affecting the logic in the executable statements. For example, use

```
const
    MAXITEMNUM  = 100;
    EPSILON     = 0.001;
    CONTROLCHAR = '@';
    ...
NUMHITS := 0;
for I := 1 to MAXITEMNUM do
    if A[I] < EPSILON then
        NUMHITS := NUMHITS + 1;
    ...
```

rather than

```
NUMHITS := 0;
  for I := 1 to 100 do
    if (A[I] < 0.001) then
        NUMHITS := NUMHITS + 1;
    ...
```

118

[Dcl-2]   *All types must be named.*

The rationale here is to be clear about the use of types. Instead of

```
var
    LEFTJUMP: array[MINSQ..MAXSQ] of
                    record
                        SQ1: INTEGER;
                        SQ2: INTEGER
                    end;
```

use

```
type
    MOVEPAIR =
        record
            SQ1: INTEGER;
            SQ2: INTEGER
        end;
    ADJACENTSQS =
        array [MINSQ..MAXSQ] of MOVEPAIR;
var
    LEFTJUMP: ADJACENTSQS;
```

This rule forces a uniformity and simplicity that ultimately saves a good deal of time.

[Dcl-3]   *No function may change the values of its arguments.*

The rationale here is to force a pure use of functions called within expressions; that is, to eliminate side effects within functions. For example, the function

```
function OCCURS (SEARCHCHAR: CHAR;
                 CHARSTR   : STRING;
                 STRLENGTH : INTEGER;
                 var ERROR : BOOLEAN): {returns} INTEGER;
    ...
    if (COUNT > STRLENGTH) then
        begin
```

119

```
                    ERROR  := TRUE;
                    OCCURS := 0
              end
          else
              begin
                    ERROR  := FALSE;
                    OCCURS := COUNT
              end;
          ...
      end;
```

is not allowed. Instead, a procedure must be used.

[Dcl-4]　　*The parameters of a procedure should be declared with comments describing the logical role of each parameter.*

The rationale here is to give some minimal information on the logical role of the procedure. For example, use

```
procedure EXAMPLE ({in}          A, B: INTEGER;
                   {in-out} var C, D: INTEGER;
                   {out}    var E, F: REAL);
```

The comments {in}, {in-out}, and {out} may be replaced by more informative comments—{using}, {updating}, and {giving}.

[Dcl-5]　　*Each field in a record should be declared separately.*

This is a small point. It means use

```
record
    ALPHA: INTEGER;
    BETA : INTEGER
end
```

not

```
record
    ALPHA, BETA: INTEGER
end
```

120

or even worse

```
record ALPHA, BETA: INTEGER end
```

I find it hard to understand the rationale for the other alternatives.

[Dcl-6] *The keywords CONST, TYPE, and VAR should occupy a line by themselves.*

This means using

```
type
    COLPOS = 1..72;
var
    COUNT: INTEGER;
    COL  : COLPOS;
```

not the more condensed

```
type COLPOS = 1..72;
var COUNT: INTEGER;
        COL:    COLPOS;
```

The rationale is to think of constants, types, and variables as "sections," introduced by a keyword.

[Dcl-7] *The bodies of constant, type, and variable declarations must be indented from the beginning of the corresponding header keywords.*

This means using

```
var
    COUNT: INTEGER;
    STACK: ITEMCOLLECTION;
```

not

```
var
COUNT: INTEGER;
STACK: ITEMCOLLECTION;
```

121

CONTROL STRUCTURES

[Control-1] *Goto's are not allowed.*

The rationale here is to force the programmers to *think ahead* and use only 1-in, 1-out control structures. Many programmers at first believe that this restriction is unreasonable. With some practice, programming with these control structures becomes quite easy. If it seems necessary to use a goto in another setting, the following alternatives should be considered:

1. *Restructuring the algorithm*

2. *Putting blocks of code in a subroutine*

3. *Copying in a piece of code*

4. *Repeating a condition previously tested*

5. *Reversing a condition to its negative.*

[Control-2] *Nesting of any combination of If, For, While, With, Case, and Repeat statements must be no more than four levels deep. A generalized case statement simulating a "select-first" is counted as one level.*

The rationale here is to prevent the human complexity that results from deeply nested control structures. If statements that simulate a generalized case statement are conceptually one level. For example,

```
if case-1 then
    statement-1
else if case-2 then
    statement-2
    ...
else if case-n then
    statement-n
```

counts as one level of nesting. It is surprising how easily this generally accepted rule is broken.

[Control-3] *Null statements must include a comment line.*

For example

```
{do nothing}
```

For example, use

```
case I of
  1: DOTHIS;
  2: X := X + 1;
  3: WRITE(X);
  4: {no action}
end
```

The rationale here is to make a null action explicit.

[Control-4] *Compound While and For statements are displayed similarly to repeat statements.*

This means using

```
while (X < Y) do begin
  statement-1;
  statement-2;
  statement-3
end

for I := 1 to NUMITEMS do begin
  statement-1;
  statement-2;
  statement-3
end

repeat
  statement-1;
  statement-2;
  statement-3
until EOF(INFILE)
```

The rationale is to give loops a parallel form and to minimize indentation. Most people don't do it. Try it.

[Control-5] *If statements are displayed in a comblike fashion rather than a nested fashion.*

I can't figure out how to say this in any clear way, but it means using this:

```
if WEATHER = SUNNY then begin  { -- single choice }
   FINISHCHORES;
   OVEN := OFF;
   TAKEABREAK
end

if WEATHER = SUNNY then begin  { -- binary choice }
   FINISHCHORES;
   OVEN := OFF;
   TAKEABREAK
end else begin
   CLEARKITCHEN;
   OVEN := ON;
   STARTCOOKING
end

if WEATHER = SUNNY then          { -- another possibility }
   begin
      FINISHCHORES;
      TAKEABREAK
   end
else
   begin
      CLEARKITCHEN;
      OVEN := ON;
      STARTCOOKING
   end
```

There is no real optimum layout for Pascal. The rationale is to prevent tricky indentation.

[Control-6] *The bodies of Begin-End, For, Repeat, While, With, and Case statements, as well as the bodies of record-end structures, must be indented from their corresponding header and closing keywords.*

This prohibits

```
begin
   X := 1;
   Y := 1
end
```

and

```
while CH <> SPACE do READ (CH)
```

and

```
record
   X: INTEGER;
   Y: INTEGER end;
```

The rationale is to force a consistent layout.

SPACING

[Space-1]   *A uniform indentation of three spaces is to be used.*

Programmers vary their indentation conventions all over the lot, which is senseless. Three spaces is perfect, and lovely for the reader. Examples are:

```
var                    { -- Case 1. Variables }
   SUM: INTEGER;

record                 { -- Case 2. Record fields }
   A: REAL;
   B: REAL
end

if (X > Y) then        { -- Case 3. Then-part }
   WRITE (X, Y)

begin                  { -- Case 4. Compound statement }
   DOTHIS;
   DOTHAT
end
```

125

```
while (X > Z) do begin    { -- Case 5. Loops }
   COUNT := COUNT + 1;
   X := X + F(X)
end
```

[Space-2] *At least one space is put before and after "=", ":=", and each relational operator.*

Obvious? No. You will often see

```
X:=X+1
```

or

if (X=Y) **then**. . .

But the problem gets worse in

```
NEWITEMCOUNT:=NEWITEMCOUNT+1
```

and

```
if (NEXTAPPROX(X,Y,EPSILON)>1.0) then...
```

The rule is ever so simple, almost a courtesy to the reader. It is not worth breaking.

[Space-3] *At least one space is put after each ":" in declarations.*

This means writing

```
A: INTEGER;
```

or

```
X : INTEGER;
X1: INTEGER;
```

but not

```
X :INTEGER;
```

The rationale is to treat the colon as in English prose, where there is always a space after it. Note that the colon is *not* an operator, which is why

```
ALPHA : INTEGER;
```

is not recommended.

[Space-4]   *At least one space is put after each ":" and ";" in parameter lists.*

This means, write

```
GETMOVE (PLAYER: PARTICIPANT; var MOVE: MOVEPAIR);
```

not

```
GETMOVE (PLAYER:PARTICIPANT ;var MOVE;MOVEPAIR);
```

The rationale is, again, to reflect normal English usage.

[Space-5]   *A space should be used as in normal English usage.*

It's elementary, but violated all the time. The rule applies to cases like

```
{--Full line comments
 --and their continuation.}

for X:=+10 ...
```

which are better written as

```
{ -- Full line comments
  -- and their continuation. }

for X := +10...
```

6 *POTPOURRI*

*A LITTLE LEARNING IS A DANGEROUS
THING; DRINK DEEP, OR TASTE NOT THE
PIERIAN SPRING.*

*Alexander Pope
Essay on Criticism, Part I*

The five topics discussed in this chapter:

> global variables,
> selecting mnemonic names,
> recursion,
> efficiency, and
> the case against program flowcharts

should not mislead the reader as being secondary to the proverbs of Chapter 2. Nor should the title "potpourri" be taken as though these vital topics are afterthoughts in the issues of Pascal programming today. On the contrary, a separate chapter is needed because these topics require and deserve a deeper discussion than the more succinct vehicle of the proverbs allows.

GLOBAL VARIABLES

The use of variables to represent updated entities is familiar to all programmers. Guidelines for the effective use of variables are seldom discussed. Nevertheless, this topic is of paramount importance.

In what follows, I am going to make some rather strong statements against the use of global variables. This is a controversial area. Before we get going, I would like to make a point that gets to the heart of this book. It is about the nature of how people read and comprehend programs.

Consider any "block" of code (i.e., a sequence of statements), B. The block B performs some computation, F, on two variables, x1 and x2, to yield a result, y, as illustrated in Figure 30. In any such block there may, of course, be other intermediate variables needed for the computation. Assume for the moment that each of the intermediate variables is not used outside the block of code B except for one variable, v. In order to abstract the computation F in B, one must then not only consider the computation of y from x1 and x2, but *also* consider the effect on v. Our simple mental model is lost. In this case we say that v is "active in" or "global to" the block.

The use of global variables is a frequent cause of complexity in computer programs. To abstract the computation of a logical block of code, the uses of global variables must be considered.

There are several problems associated with global variables. First, the complexity of a block of statements rapidly increases with even a small increase in the number of variables. Second, if the number of statements over which the variables range is large, then the intent of referencing statements can be difficult to comprehend. Third, any change to a program outside the block of statements can affect the correctness of the block itself.

The concept of global variables in Pascal is most evident in the case of variables that are external to a function or procedure. The examples which follow take advantage of this circumstance. But the concept should be understood in terms of *any* block of code that has the *effect* of a unit of computation.

Pascal is careful to make the following (commonly held) distinction. A "function" refers to a subprogram that returns a value. A "procedure" refers to a subprogram that produces a change in a variable outside the subprogram. In particular, consider the simple declaration of Figure 31. In Figure 31(a), the subprogram AREA is used as a function. For example, if the value of R is 3.0, an evaluation of the expression

```
1.0 + AREA(R)
```

yields one, plus the value of the function. In Figure 31(b), the subprogram AREA is used as a procedure. For example, if the value of R is 3.0, the statement

```
GETAREA (R, AREA)
```

results in assigning to AREA the value computed by the procedure. The difference between functions and procedures is important but not always obvious. Generally speaking,

• functions are used in place of *expressions* to return *values*,

whereas,

• procedures are used in place of *statements* to perform *assignments* to variables.

Figure 30.   **Mental abstraction**

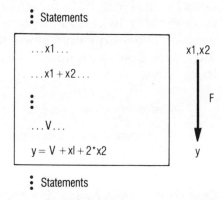

Figure 31.   ***Functions versus procedures***

(a) A Simple Function

```
function AREA(RADIUS: REAL): REAL;
   const
       PI = 3.14159;
begin
   AREA := PI * (RADIUS*RADIUS)
end;
```

(b) A Simple Procedure

```
procedure GETAREA(RADIUS: REAL; var AREA: REAL);
   const
      PI = 3.14159;
begin
   AREA := PI * (RADIUS*RADIUS)
end;
```

It is possible in Pascal to write subprograms that both return a value and cause an effect outside the subprogram. As a rule, it is unwise to do this, as we shall see in subsequent examples.

Context Effects

Loosely speaking, the *context* of a subprogram (i.e., function or procedure) is its relation to other sections of a program. If a function alters a quantity global to itself, then it exhibits a *context effect*. Basically a function can produce a context effect in three ways:

1. *by altering its arguments*

2. *by altering a global variable*

3. *by using a global variable that is changed between calls.*

Case (2) is known as a "side effect." In case (3), not at all harmless, the damage comes from outside the function.

Programmers who write functions with context effects can get unpleasant surprises. Consider Figure 32. These two program segments are identical except for the replacement of the expression

```
F(B) + F(B)
```

in Figure 32(a) by the expression

```
2.0*F(B)
```

in Figure 32(b). These two programs are not equivalent because

```
F(B) + F(B) = (11)*(3) + (12)*(3)
            = 69

2*F(B)      = (2)*(11)*(3)
            = 66
```

Figure 32.   *Context effect on the returned value of a function*

(a) One Program

```
program ADDITION1 (INPUT, OUTPUT);
   var
       A, B, C: INTEGER;

function F(X: INTEGER): INTEGER;
begin
   A := A + 1;
   F := A * X
end;

begin
   A := 10;
   B := 3;
   C := F(B) + F(B);   { -- use of F }
   WRITELN (C)
end.
```

(b) An Equivalent Program?

```
program ADDITION2 (INPUT, OUTPUT);
   var
       A, B, C: INTEGER;

function F(X: INTEGER): INTEGER;
begin
   A := A + 1;
   F := A * X
end;
```

```
begin
   A := 10;
   B := 3;
   C := 2 * F(B);   { -- use of F }
   WRITELN (C)
end.
```

Hence we lose a fundamental property of addition. The problem is caused by the context effect in the function F with the assignment of (A + 1) to A, where A is global to the function.

A similar case arises in Figure 33. These examples are also identical except that

```
F(B) + G(B)
```

in Figure 33(a) is replaced by

```
G(B) + F(B)
```

in Figure 33(b). Using a left-to-right evaluation, the written values for C, 72 and 75, are not the same. Here the familiar commutative property of addition is lost because of the assignment to a global variable. Certainly many programmers would be surprised to learn that F(B) + G(B) is not equivalent to G(B) + F(B). Since Pascal employs conventional mathematical notation, it is dangerous to write functions that violate the properties of established mathematical systems.

Figure 33.   *Context effect by assignment to a global variable*

(a) One Program

```
program ADDITION3 (INPUT, OUTPUT);
   var
      A, B, C: INTEGER;

function F(X: INTEGER): INTEGER;
begin
   A := A + 1;
   F := A * X
end;
```

```
function G(X: INTEGER): INTEGER;
begin
  A := A + 2;
  G := A * X
end;

begin
  A := 10;
  B := 3;
  C := F(B) + G(B);   { -- calls to F and G }
  WRITELN (C)
end.
```

(b) An Equivalent Program

```
program ADDITION4 (INPUT, OUTPUT);
  var
      A, B, C: INTEGER;

function F(X: INTEGER): INTEGER;
begin
  A := A + 1;
  F := A * X
end;

function G(X: INTEGER): INTEGER;
begin
  A := A + 2;
  G := A * X
end;

begin
  A := 10;
  B := 3;
  C := G(B) + F(B);   { -- calls to F and G }
  WRITELN (C)
end.
```

Next consider Figure 34, a case in which a function sub-program alters the value of an argument. The problem here is that two function calls with the same arguments return *different* values. In larger programs, such a use of arguments is quite dangerous. In making a correction or alteration, the programmer may unwittingly alter the value of calls to the function.

Furthermore, to replace F with another procedure, the programmer must consider the main program in order to ensure the proper handling of global variables.

Last, consider Figure 35, where a similar thing happens, only here the effect comes from *outside* the function. It's the same problem.

Figure 34.   **Context effect on the arguments of a function**

```pascal
program SIDEEFFECT (INPUT, OUTPUT);
  var
     A, B, C: INTEGER;

function F(X: INTEGER; var Y: INTEGER): INTEGER;
begin
   Y := Y + X;
   F := X * Y
end;

begin
  A := 4;
  B := F(2, A);   { -- gives 12 }
  C := F(2, A);   { -- gives 16 }
  WRITELN (B, C)
end.
```

Figure 35.   **Context effect from outside a subprogram**

```pascal
program TROUBLE (INPUT, OUTPUT);
  var
     A, B, C: INTEGER;

function F(X: INTEGER): INTEGER;
begin
   F := X * A;
end;

begin
  A := 1;
  B := 2;
  C := F(B);   { -- gives 2 }
  WRITELN (C);

  A := 2;
  C := F(B);   { -- gives 4 }
  WRITELN (C);
end.
```

The purpose of a procedure is to produce some effect external to itself, not to return a value. Essentially, a procedure consists of a group of statements isolated from a main routine or program for convenience or clarity. The problems encountered with context effects in procedures are quite similar to those encountered in functions. There is one important exception. Since a procedure is designed to update a specific set of variables, each of the changed variables should be included in the list of arguments. Consider Figure 36. By using all assigned variables in the argument list in each procedure call, the reader can speed up tracing the changed variables, since he or she will not have to look through the body of the procedure.

Figure 36.   *Context effect in procedures*

(a) Poor

```
program HIDDENPARAMETER (INPUT, OUTPUT);
    var
        A, B: INTEGER;

procedure P (var X: INTEGER);
begin
    X := 2 * (X + 1);
    B := 5 * X
end;

begin
    A := 17;
    B := 3;
    P(A);
    WRITELN (A, B)    { -- B is not 3 }
end.
```

(b) Better

```
program EXPLICITPARAMETER (INPUT, OUTPUT);
    var
        A, B: INTEGER;

procedure P (var X, Y: INTEGER);
```

```
begin
  X := 2 * (X + 1);
  Y := 5 * X
end;
begin
  A := 17;
  B := 3;
  P(A, B);   { -- tells about B }
  WRITELN (A, B)
end.
```

The case against context effects becomes even more severe when we need to change a program. Change is a daily occurrence in programming. Someone may find a more efficient algorithm, more output may be needed, a bug may be detected, or revised specifications may be given. If a piece of code to be changed has context effects, then those effects must be accounted for. The resulting changes may imply the need to delve deeply into the entire program for a clear understanding of what effects a function or procedure has on other parts of the program. Adding a few extra lines of code for that desirable change may kill the correctness of another piece of code. As a result, another change may be needed to right matters, and so on. Even if this process succeeds, it is not likely to add to the clarity or flexibility of the program. Had the original program been written without context effects, the subprogram could be changed *without* looking at the rest of the program.

There are, of course, cases where global entities may indeed be useful. For example, there may be arrays whose (often used) values remain constant within the program. Making these quantities global to the entire program certainly causes no problems. The global use of the legal move mappings in the Kriegspiel program illustrates this point. These are *not* really global variables, but global *constants*.

Global variables and context effects can cause serious problems. If they are used, they should be used sparingly. In summary, I give the following rules of thumb:

1. **Functions**
   Do not use a function when you need a procedure.
   Use a function only for its returned value.
   Do not alter formal parameters.
   Do not use any global variables.

2. Procedures

Do not use a procedure when you need a function.
Do not use global variables.
Put all outside variables in the parameter list.

3. Both

Be very careful if you ever use global variables.

SELECTING MNEMONIC NAMES

When writing Pascal programs, it is tempting to use short and often uninformative user-defined names. An extra effort is required to devise and actually code more illuminating (but not always longer) names. Nevertheless, the choice of names has a long-lasting impact that cannot be ignored. Consider the two toy programs in Figure 37. Of the two, Figure 37(b) is the more lucid procedure for reading a sequence of numeric values and printing the maximum.

Good mnemonic names are a powerful tool for clear documentation, easy verification, and ready maintenance. We offer several basic principles for devising user-defined names:

1. *Choose names that activate the correct "meaning" or "psychological set" [see Weinberg, 1971].*

2. *Try to use short, full names.*

3. *Use standard names and abbreviations.*

4. *Follow consistent naming conventions.*

5. *Avoid names that can be confused with a system name, that are unpronounceable, or that are otherwise incomprehensible.*

Figure 37.   *Using mnemonic names*

(a) Poor

```
program BIG (INPUT, OUTPUT);
    var
        N, INDEX: INTEGER;
        X, BIG  : REAL;
```

```
begin
    WRITE ('Enter length of sequence: ');
    READLN (N);
    WRITE ('Enter first number: ');
    READLN (X);
    BIG := X;
    for INDEX := 1 to N do begin
        WRITE ('Next number: ');
        READLN (X);
        if BIG < X then
            BIG := X
    end;
    WRITELN ('The largest value = ', BIG)
end.
```

(b) Better

```
program MAX (INPUT, OUTPUT);
    var
        NUMVALUES, I: INTEGER;
        N, MAXVALUE:  REAL;

begin
    WRITE ('Enter length of sequence: ');
    READLN (NUMVALUES);
    WRITE ('Enter first number: ');
    READLN (N);
    MAXVALUE := N;
    for I := 1 to NUMVALUES do begin
        WRITE ('Next number: ');
        READLN (N);
        if MAXVALUE < N then
            MAXVALUE := N
    end;
    WRITELN ('The largest value = ', MAXVALUE)
end.
```

Meaning

In psychology, the term *psychological set* (see Weinberg, 1971, in the Bibliography) means a readiness to respond in a specific way to certain stimuli. In the programming context, a "psychological set" means a readiness to associate particular entities or properties with a word. Entities such as social security numbers, rates of pay, and people's names have many possible word representations. It is important that the psychological set activated by a particular name be "correct" (i.e., represent the intended entity). Of course, the psychological set activated by a particular name differs for different people.

We start with a simple example. Suppose you use the identifier

```
NCHAR
```

in a program. What would you think? Hmm? Some possibilities are

1. *the number of characters?*

2. *a number for a character?*

3. *an n-character array?*

Right off, you say the name is poor. Now what about

```
GETCOORD
```

Looks better. It is probably a procedure to get a coordinate.

But there is a big point here. Programmers should always choose names that activate the precise meaning. Some rules are:

1. *Decide* exactly *what is to be named.*

2. *Choose a name that says it.*

3. *Look at the name as it appears in the code and ask if the reader will be able to conclude the same thing.*

Rule C is the key. When you read something like

```
if A[NCHAR] = B[COUNT] then ...
```

chances are you have problems. But when you see something like

```
GETCOORD(XPOSITION, YPOSITION)
```

141

or

```
if COUNT[NEXTCHAR] = MAXALLOWED then...
```

the going is probably a lot easier. This is what naming is all about.

Creating a name with the correct psychological set can be difficult. Often it is easy to pick a name with a close but dangerously incorrect psychological set. As an example, suppose a programmer decided to represent a file of sale transaction items, and the record's three fields (the identification of the salesperson, the identification of the item sold, and the quantity of the item sold) with the respective names TRANSFILE, FIELD1, FIELD2, and FIELD3. The name TRANSFILE might cause a reader to associate the following

1. *a transit file*

2. *transactions of any sort*

3. *transportation records*

and so on. A better choice would be SALEFILE, and even better, SALESFILE or SALESDATA. Likewise, the data names FIELD1, FIELD2, and FIELD3 are less clear than PERSONID, ITEMID, and NUMSOLD.

Short, Full Names

If possible, keep the names of programs short and full. If the program is about the game of checkers, it is unnecessary to use the names CHECKERCOUNT, CHECKERSQ, and CHECKER-MOVE when COUNT, SQ, and MOVE will do.

Another aspect of naming arises when names have no specific semantic role. For example, a programmer may define an array whose subscripts do not correspond to any meaningful object in the real world, or he may define a function of purely mathematical arguments. In both cases, a standard name should be used. For example, subscripts are generally denoted by I, J, or K; functions by F, G, or H; and arguments by X, Y, or Z. Often these familiar conventions will lend understanding. For example,

```
I = F(X, Y)
```

is more suggestive than

```
Y = X(I, F)
```

if the left-hand side denotes an integer-valued variable and the right-hand side denotes the application of a function to two arbitrary real variables.

A name that is an abbreviation for a longer conceptual unit can also be hazardous, especially when the resulting abbreviation is just plain confusing. For example, a programmer who desires a name for a rate of pay entry would be unwise to use the name ROPE, which does not semantically reflect the entity's true value. The temptation, of course, is to think of a heavy cord of intertwined fibers. Other poor choices are

PENTRY	strange
RPAY	cryptic
PAYAMT	amount to be paid?
RATEENTRY	vacuous
SALARY	usually not an hourly rate
RATEOFPAYPERHOUR	too long
WAGE	not specific enough

Good choices might be PAYRATE or HOURLYWAGE. These are good, short, full names.

Words like FIELD1, FIELD2, and FIELD3 should be avoided for still another reason. Suppose that the format of a transaction was changed so that the salesperson identification number became the third field instead of the first field, and the item sold number became the first instead of the second field, etc. The word FIELD1 must then be changed to FIELD3, FIELD2 to FIELD1, etc. Needless to say, it is highly possible that some occurrence of the word FIELD3 might not be changed to FIELD1! Finding a mistake like the printer just made in the last sentence is another problem with such words.

Remember, you should only abbreviate after you have created a full mnemonic name. The chosen abbreviation should not activate a psychological set different from the original name.

Let us assume you have created the lengthy mnemonic name OWNER-IDENTIFICATION-NUMBER and that it activates the correct psychological set. Even though you must abbreviate the name, you should reject such abbreviations as OND or OWNID, for they may very well be misleading. A word like IDNUM is preferable. Admittedly, a good solution to the problem is hard to devise, and ultimately depends on the context of the program itself.

Standard Names and Abbreviations

We encourage the adoption of a full set of standard names and abbreviations for every major programming application. For programmers working on a team or modifying someone else's code, the value of standard mnemonics is obvious. Even if you are a student, your instructor may wish to choose standard names for an assignment to simplify understanding of everyone's program.

A formal set of standard names and abbreviations makes the selection of names easy. If your instructor, customer, or programming manager wants an input record to have the name MASTER, or a value on a graph to have the name YCOORD, then these are the "best" names to use, for they make a program consistent with established conventions.

If you have no formal set of standard names or abbreviations, informal standard names and abbreviations are often available. In the case of a grading program, names like SCORE, GRADE, or MEAN are illuminating informal standards. Furthermore, Pascal programmers have their own familiar conventions, for example:

SUM	For summing elements in an array
IDNUM	For identification numbers
DENOM	For denominators of fractions
AVE	For averages
ERROR	For error flags
TOTALERROR	For total accumulated error values
EPSILON	For error tolerances

The use of words such as these makes a program consistent with informal conventions.

As for standard abbreviations, a good place to start is a dictionary. The Pascal limitation to names without a break character makes abbreviations sometimes confusing. Despite this awkward inconvenience, you must make sure that abbreviations are well understood. What better place to start than your dictionary?

Abbreviations and short names are a much more important issue than they appear. Long-winded names are tiresome to type, boring to read, and can upset good program layout. Imagine reading a program with many occurrences of

```
CUSTOMERIDENTIFICATIONNUMBER
```

when, perhaps,

```
IDNUM
```

will do the trick. You see, the key is to choose those names that

1. *can be shortened easily, and*

2. *are frequently used.*

These are the names that count. The point here is *not* to abbreviate uncommon words or those that can confuse. Compare

```
RUNAVERAGE  vs.  RUNNINGAVE
SUMREPORT   vs.  SUMMARYRPT
NCHARACTER  vs.  NEXTCHAR
PLYRNUMBER  vs.  PLAYERNUM
```

The column on the right is superior because the *familiar* part is abbreviated.

Other Considerations

In addition to finding a proper name for each entity, you should choose names that fit well in the program as a whole. Consider the following pairs of names.

Name for One Entity	Name for Another Entity	Difference
(a) BKRPNT	BRKPNT	Almost invisible
(b) LISTACTION	.ACTIONLIST	Verb versus noun
(c) GETCODE	CODE	Verb versus noun
(d) IDEN	IDENT	Small
(e) OMEGA	DELTA	Large
(f) ROOT	DISCRIMINANT	Large and informative

In this table the difference between pairs of names is suggestive of differences in meaning. Entry (a) shows two discrete names, but in a program could you be sure that one is not a typing or keypunching error? In general, shy away from using "close" names.

Entries (b) and (c) suggest that one might represent a procedure, the other a (noun) argument. Entry (d) is odd, indicative of a subtle difference in the programmer's (not the reader's) mind. Entries (e) and (f) are fine—short, informative, full names.

Consider the following four function names, which are taken from an actual program. The names had the following meanings:

Name (Argument)	Meaning
MOVLF(SQ1)	MOVE Left From square SQ1
MOVLT(SQ1)	MOVE Left To square SQ1
MOVRF(SQ1)	MOVE Right From square SQ1
MOVRT(SQ1)	MOVE Right To square SQ1

The programmer, in this case, wrote four functions that required a square on a checkerboard as an argument. The input square was denoted by SQ1, and the value returned by the function was TRUE or FALSE, depending on whether it was possible to move left or right, from or to, the square SQ1 given as input. The choice of names, good on initial consideration, resulted in a series of errors. The programmer unfortunately confused MOVLF and MOVRF. It *literally* took days to discover this mistake.

A programmer should also be sure that all user-defined names exhibit "uniformity." This is also a difficult notion to formalize. In rough terms, all user-defined names that imply similar properties should be of similar form. For example, consider the previous maximum value example. It would be unfortunate to choose the names

    NUM
    NEXT
    BIGVAL

Even though they can suggest the correct meaning, the names do not follow a uniform coding scheme. A better choice of names is

    NUMVALUES
    NEXTVAL
    MAXVAL

The programmer is especially advised to keep abbreviations uniform.

In a similar vein, consider the following names:

    XX1   *why 2 x's?*
    FNXD   *cryptic*
    CRDTE   *unpronounceable*
    FLAG   *not informative*

These are all unfortunate.

Finally, before using a name in a program, the programmer should also make sure that it is not a system name or a Pascal keyword. It is handy to keep a list of keywords and a list of system names.

Let us put it this way.

1. *Look at the code (not the declaration) to see if a name works.*

2. *Rely on context to pick a short name that still suggest the correct meaning.*

3. *Only if necessary, abbreviate.*

RECURSION

Loosely speaking, recursion is a method of definition in which the object being defined is used within the definition. For example, consider the following definition of the word "descendant":

> A descendant of a person is a son or daughter of the person, or a descendant of a son or daughter.

In this definition *all* the descendants of the person are simply and precisely accounted for. A nonrecursive definition of "descendant" that takes all possibilities into consideration would be the following:

> A descendant of a person is a son or daughter of the person, or a grandson or granddaughter of the person, or a great-grandson or great-granddaughter of the person, etc.

In this case, the definition is lengthier and less succinct than the recursive definition. It is interesting to note how dictionaries attempt to skirt recursion in the definition of "descendant." "Descendant" is often defined in terms of "ancestor," whereas "ancestor" is defined in terms of "descendant." The two definitions are, in fact, mutually recursive.

In programming, recursive definitions apply to function and procedure declarations. A recursive subprogram declaration is one that has the potential to invoke itself. In other words, it is defined partially in terms of itself.

The primary point of this section is that in many instances recursive definitions are clearer, more succinct, or more natural, than their nonrecursive counterparts, even if they are less efficient. Recursive definitions often follow naturally using the top-down programming approach. A clear idea of the nature and power of recursive definitions can be a valuable aid to a Pascal programmer, especially when pointer structures or treelike solutions are used.

Suppose we wish to sum the elements of an integer array. Simple arithmetic gives us the following equality:

```
SUM (A, n) = A[1]                   if n = 1
SUM (A, n) = A[n] + SUM (A, n-1)    if n >= 2
```

Stated in English, the sum of the elements of an array is the last element plus the sum of the first n − 1 elements. If the array has only one element, the sum is the single element. With these facts in mind, it is possible to write the function SUM recursively, as in Figure 38(a). Its nonrecursive counterpart is given in Figure 38(b). (Note: Figure 38(a) is used for simplicity of illustration. It is not a good idea to write recursive solutions for simple iteration.)

To ensure that the recursive definition of SUM is understood, observe the following analysis of the function subprogram when applied to a four-element array containing the numbers 3, 6, 8, and 2.

Depth of Recursive Calls	Value of SUM
1	SUM(A, 4)
2	2 + SUM(A, 3)
3	2 + (8 + SUM(A, 2))
4	2 + (8 + (6 + SUM(A, 1)))
4	2 + (8 + (6 + 3))
3	2 + (8 + 9)
2	2 + 17
1	19

Figure 38. ***Summation defined with and without recursion***

(a) Recursive Definition

```
type
    INTARRAY = array [1..100] of INTEGER;

function SUM(A: INTARRAY; N: INTEGER): INTEGER;
begin
    if N = 1 then
        SUM := A[1]
    else
        SUM := A[N] + SUM(A, N-1)
end;
```

(b) Nonrecursive Definition

```
type
    INTARRAY = array [1..100] of INTEGER;

function SUM(A: INTARRAY;  N: INTEGER): INTEGER;
    var
        I: INTEGER;
begin
    SUM := 0;
    for I := 1 to N do
        SUM := SUM + A[I]
end;
```

An example better suited to recursive definition is the implementation of Euclid's algorithm for computing the greater common divisor of two positive integers, M and N. The GCD function subprogram requires an additional integer function **mod** that returns the remainder when I is divided by J.

The definitions are shown in Figure 39. For comparison, a nonrecursive definition for the same function subprogram is also given. The nonrecursive definitions are slightly larger and less clear. The properties of the algorithm are still present, but they are hidden by the looping constructs.

Merely knowing what recursion looks like is not enough. It is also necessary to know (1) if recursion is applicable to the problem at hand, and (2) how to apply it. There are no formal rules in either case, but there are some guidelines. One is that the notion of mathematical "induction" is a close analogy to recursion. Induction is a method of definition in which (1) initial values of a function are defined explicitly (the base step), and (2) other values are implicitly defined in terms of previous values (the inductive step). If the definition given in the second step applies to all elements other than the initial values, then the principle of mathematical induction asserts that the function is (explicitly) well-defined for all values in its domain.

To illustrate the method of inductive definition, consider the sequence of Fibonacci numbers. The first two numbers are both 1, and each successive number in the sequence is the sum of the two preceding numbers. More explicitly,

$N = 1$ Base Step $\qquad F(1) = 1$

$N = 2$ $\qquad F(2) = 1$

$N \geq 3$ Inductive Step $\qquad F(N) = F(N-1) + F(N-2)$

Figure 39.	***Euclid's algorithm defined with and without recursion***

(a) Recursive Definition

```
function GCD(M, N: INTEGER): INTEGER;
    var
        REMAINDER: INTEGER;
begin
    if M < N then
        GCD := GCD(N, M)
    else
        begin
            REMAINDER := M mod N;
            if REMAINDER = 0 then
                GCD := N
            else
                GCD := GCD(N, REMAINDER)
        end
end;
```

(b) Nonrecursive Definition

```
function GCD(M, N: INTEGER): INTEGER;
    var
        REMAINDER, LOVALUE, HIVALUE: INTEGER;
begin
    HIVALUE := MAX(M, N);
    LOVALUE := MIN(M, N);
    REMAINDER := HIVALUE mod LOVALUE;
    if REMAINDER = 0 then
        GCD := LOVALUE
    else
        begin
            repeat
                REMAINDER := HIVALUE mod LOVALUE;
                HIVALUE   := LOVALUE;
                LOVALUE   := REMAINDER
            until (REMAINDER = 0);
            GCD := HIVALUE
        end
end;
```

The step from this inductive definition to a recursive function declaration is small. A function subprogram to generate the *n*th Fibonacci number is shown defined recursively and nonrecursively in Figure 40. The Fibonacci function written recursively parrots the inductive definition and clearly shows the main property of the Fibonacci numbers. While the nonrecursive example uses the same property, it is harder to detect. The additional code required to write the function nonrecursively is mostly bookkeeping. Also note that in the recursive definition, the function subprogram FIB is recursively invoked twice. Without a good optimizing compiler, this double invocation is quite inefficient.

Figure 40.   *The Fibonacci sequence*

(a) Recursive Definition

```
function FIB(N: INTEGER): INTEGER;
begin
   if N <= 2 then
      FIB := 1
   else
      FIB := FIB(N-1) + FIB(N-2)
end;
```

(b) Nonrecursive Definition

```
function FIB(N: INTEGER): INTEGER;
   var
      F1, F2, I, TEMP: INTEGER;
begin
   if N <= 2 then
      FIB := 1
   else
      begin
         F1 := 1;
         F2 := 1;
         for I := 3 to N do begin
            TEMP := F1 + F2;
            F1   := F2;
            F2   := TEMP;
            FIB  := TEMP
         end
      end
end;
```

A good deal could be said about recursion, and a good deal of the literature is devoted to the subject. For our purposes, the point is simple. Understand the use of recursion and the translation from a recursive definition to a nonrecursive Pascal code. You may find that recursion is a valuable addition to your programming skills.

EFFICIENCY

Machine efficiency has been one of the most frequent concerns of managers, instructors, and programmers alike. In the early years of computing, when hardware configurations were small and slow, it was important to use as little storage space or computer time as possible. Since then, digital computers have become more powerful, inexpensive, and fast. Yet there is still frequent concern with the question of machine efficiency because of the need to control programming costs.

The reasons for striving for machine efficiency are not only historic and economic; there is also a certain human element. Programmers take pride in their ability to squeeze out excess lines of code or to use an appropriate efficiency feature, and managers take a natural pride in the speed of their programs or their compact use of storage.

The Real Costs

While we do not at all question the need to reduce programming costs, we do believe that this concern is often focused on the wrong issues. For example, some typical concerns in Pascal programming are the following:

1. *Using numerous global variables.*

2. *Avoiding procedures and functions.*

3. *Making use of goto's.*

4. *Writing if statements so that the most frequent conditions are checked first.*

These rules are intended to save space and execution time, thus lowering costs. Because of the often rather small and local savings afforded by the above techniques, we shall call the efficiency they provide "micro-efficiency" [Armstrong, 1973]. With the development of inexpensive fast storage and virtual memory systems, the preoccupation with the size and speed of machine code would seem to have been dealt a death blow. Not so! Old habits remain.

The concern with micro-efficiency has often obscured the really important programming costs. The first issue is to understand the problem completely and make sure that the resulting specification satisfies the user. The second issue is to produce high-quality system design, clear code, and clear documentation. The final issue, and only if necessary, is to produce a fast or compact program.

While micro-efficient programs do help to reduce overall costs, in the larger perspective, they are usually only a small factor. The total cost of a system includes the costs of promotion, time needed to understand user requirements, the development of clear and acceptable specifications, program writing, documentation, and above all, maintenance. If a proposed programming system is not acceptable to the ultimate user, further development is wasted. If specifications are not adequate, system development is often misdirected and delayed. If there is a failure to recognize exceptional conditions and different solution strategies or if there is a poor initial design, the success of any development effort is undermined. Moreover, program development costs include programmer training, thinking time, coding time, and the time and effort needed to integrate a subsystem into an overall system. Documentation costs include the time needed to prepare reports, figures, and summaries of existing code.

In the life of many large programs, the largest cost factor is system maintenance. Maintenance of an ill-conceived, poorly developed, poorly coded, or poorly documented system is expensive and time consuming at best. More typically, program performance is seriously degraded. Easy maintenance of itself can yield greater savings than micro-efficient program performance. To control programming costs, we must look in the right places.

Program Performance

There are, of course, cases where the costs of program performance are significant. Perhaps a given program will be run every day, a given data file may be accessed every hour, or fast memory may be scarce. In these cases, attention should be devoted to the *top* levels of program design where "macro-efficient" techniques can be applied.

It does little good to scatter time and space micro-efficiencies all over the code if the file and array organizations are not optimal. At an even higher level, file and array techniques will be of little avail if the entire program frequently needs to be restarted because of the errors due to the improper input of data. In such cases, perhaps several sequentially executed programs with local and less severe restraints should be designed and substituted for one large program. At the highest level, if the whole program is more easily handled without a digital computer, all the concern with computer performance cost is meaningless.

A rather significant issue stems from the following observation. It is estimated that 90 percent of the CPU time in a program is spent on 10 percent of the code. If a programmer is faced with program performance demands, the first consideration should be *where* the program is losing its time. Micro-efficiency can then be spent on this 10 percent of the code.

Finally, if a program is designing low-level portions of code and really needs micro-efficient techniques, caution is still in order. Considerations such as packing characters, using integer codes, or avoiding types can make a program quite machine dependent. Tight, tricky, micro-efficient code can be almost impossible for another person to understand. These performance savings may in the end raise the cost of program maintenance.

Consider Figure 41. Each element of code is designed to select the player leading the first card in a card game. Successively higher bids are represented by successively increasing integers. The four-element integer array BID contains the final bids by each of the four players. The players are numbered clockwise from one to four, and the lead player is the person to the left of the highest bidder. Notice that Figure 41(a) eliminates several lines of code. Would you use it in your card-playing program?

If you do prefer the program of Figure 41(a) to that of Figure 41(b), look at both carefully. Do you prefer the first because it executes more rapidly or requires less storage? On the computer you regularly use, you may, in fact, find that Figure 41(b) requires less storage, because the loop may take fewer instructions than the straightline code from the corresponding statement in Figure 41(a). In addition, Figure 41(b) may execute faster because no divisions or multiplications are required, and there may be fewer additions. In short, beware of "clever" code, and beware of being penny-wise and pound-foolish.

The overriding points of our discussion can be summarized as follows. The concern with program micro-efficiency is often shortsighted. The primary concern should be to consider overall program costs and to place major economic emphasis on earlier phases of program development. There is a lot of money being wasted in the production of poor definitions, poor designs, poor documentation, and in the development of slipshod programs.

And last, but not least, if someone presents a solution that is supposed to be efficient, be careful. Watch out for the rhetoric. Have a live, running demonstration. It's worth a thousand words.

THE CASE AGAINST PROGRAM FLOWCHARTS

In 1947, H.H. Goldstine and J. von Neumann [see Goldstine and von Neumann, 1963] introduced a pictorial notation called a "flow diagram." Its purpose was to facilitate the translation of algorithms into machine language programs. The flow diagrams pictured the course of machine control through a sequence of steps and indicated the contents and change of items in storage. Since then these ideas and notations, along with various diagrams and charts used in business systems analysis [Cougar, 1973], have been absorbed into almost all areas of electronic data processing. The basic concept has come to be known as "flowcharting." We can roughly distinguish between three types of flowcharts: system flowcharts, design diagrams, and program flowcharts.

Figure 41.   *Code to determine leading player*

(a) Tricky Version

```
const
   NUMPLAYERS = 4;
type
   BIDINFO = array [1..NUMPLAYERS] of INTEGER;
var
   MAX, LEADER, N: INTEGER;
   BID:            BIDINFO;

begin
   N := (BID[1] div MAX) + 2*(BID[2] div MAX)
        + 3*(BID[3] div MAX) + 4*(BID[4] div MAX);
   LEADER := 1 + (N mod NUMPLAYERS);
   WRITELN ('The leader is player number ', LEADER)
end;
```

(b) More Natural Version

```
const
   NUMPLAYERS = 4;
type
   BIDINFO = array [1..NUMPLAYERS] of INTEGER;
var
   PLAYER, BIDDER,
   MAX, LEADER: INTEGER;
   BID       : BIDINFO;

begin
   for PLAYER := 1 to NUMPLAYERS do
      if BID[PLAYER] = MAX then
         BIDDER := PLAYER;

   if BIDDER = NUMPLAYERS then
      LEADER := 1
   else
      LEADER := PLAYER + 1;
   WRITELN ('The leader is player number ', LEADER)
end;
```

System flowcharts describe the flow of major data items and the control sequence of major operations in a system. It is customary to picture the relationship existing between information, media, equipment, equipment operations, and manual operations. An example is given in Figure 42. There are few specific details, and only a rough picture of the overall process.

Another example, but more of a design diagram, is Figure 43. This suggests a broad view of an overall design. It is quick and to the point.

Figure 42.   *A system flowchart for end-of-month weather analysis*

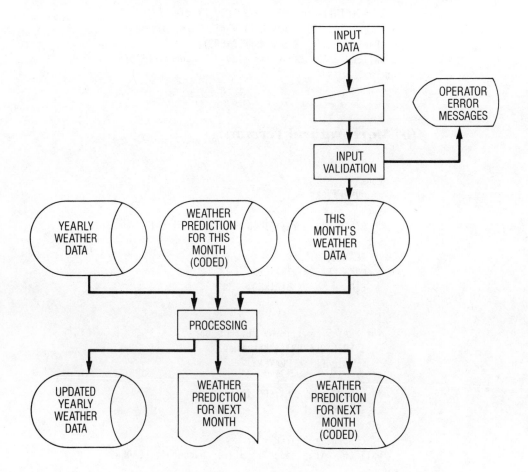

Figure 43.   *Overall design chart*

Program flowcharts, on the other hand, specify details of the sequential flow of control through an actual program. A familiar example is Figure 44. Program flowcharts are the most direct descendant of Goldstine and von Neumann's flow diagrams, for both describe the flow of control in great detail. It is interesting to note that program flowcharts do not explicitly describe the data flow, as was the case with the original flow diagrams.

As for system flowcharts and design diagrams, we believe that they can be useful aids in describing systems and processes. For documentation, they can give a quick synopsis of a process. Unfortunately, the use of these charts has sometimes been mistaken for complete problem description.

Our concern here is with program flowcharts, a technique familiar to all programmers and one often used daily. It is perhaps true that program flowcharts can assist in the design of very efficient, small algorithms. However, we believe that program flowcharts can easily suppress much useful information in favor of highlighting sequential control flow, something which distracts the programmer from the important functional relationship in the overall design. This, in turn, may obscure the use of alternative designs via the use of procedures and subprograms, the use of more intuitive data structures, or even the simple fine tuning of logic.

Figure 44.   *A program flowchart*

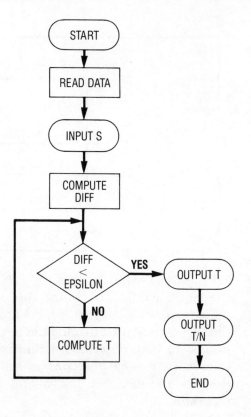

The program flowchart in Figure 44 may illustrate further the rationale for Proverb 11: Don't Goto. It is simple, but has no meaning without the program itself. Yet the shelves of books on programming are crammed with these kinds of flowcharts—many of the books for novices who are experiencing the delights of their first home computer. Is this representation useful? Perhaps it gives a visual presentation of how data is being determined, but can anyone use the flowchart itself to make a decision about the proper sequencing for coding? I think not. And as more complicated procedures are "flowcharted," a labyrinth of lines, arrows, and geometric figures results in a stillborn challenge just to interpret the flowchart itself, never mind the waste of energy in producing it. Seldom is any meaningful intelligence produced with these kinds of devices.

Consider another example, that in Figure 45. The a_1 stands for certain actions (e.g., assignments or procedure calls); the d_1 stands for decisions. The programmer who derived this flowchart was so concerned with lines and boxes (i.e., sequences of steps) that the resulting code, while correct, tends to obscure the overall functional logic.

Perhaps the inherent problem of program flowcharts is keeping track of variables that change from one part of the flowchart to the next. A user who is so preoccupied with the flow of control details misses other critical details.

Figure 45.   ***A program flowchart schema***

The value of flowcharts is easily discounted. Think back. Have you *ever* been asked to update or correct a program in which the documentation included program flowcharts? Did you consult the flowcharts before updating? Almost without exception our observations and experiences have been that during maintenance and modification of programs, flowcharts are discarded by the necessity of a careful study of the code that produced them in the first place. Code alone is sufficient for any detailed understanding needed for program maintenance.

Another criticism of program flowcharts is the ungainly way in which they always seem to spill over the margin of the paper so that with the many connectors and page turns, you seldom know where you are much less where you are going. Even when the connectors are kept to a minimum to prevent mental page turning, the mental data processing involves too many conditional checks (i.e., branches) in flowcharts. As you connect all these branches to their logical destinations, you are overwhelmed by a "spaghetti effect"—the profusion of so many crisscrossing branches.

Furthermore, if we modify a piece of code, what should be done with the program flowchart? Now we get into a process of revising more lines and boxes, perhaps inventing a color code for "Mod1" and "Mod2". If an original program is truly viable—that is, having the ability to grow and expand—the accompanying program flowchart must be modified as the program coding is changed. After a few years and many modifications, one may have an interesting, modernistic work of art but a doubtfully useful flowchart. Even if a flowchart generator is available as modifications are made, I have found that flowchart generators do not produce a more helpful flowchart for future use than the original one was for the current modification.

In summary, if we look at the various stages of the programming process, the utility of program flowcharts has no meaning in development, documentation, coding, testing, and debugging. And I believe that program flowcharts have a negative effect in maintenance and modification. Simply put, why do we devote talent and energy to something that we do not trust? Programmers and managers should think twice before using time and resources for constructing program flowcharts, no matter what part of the programming process they are designed for. For good program design, we recommend the top-down approach, which is discussed in Chapter 7.

EXERCISES FOR PART II

Exercise 1   *Mnemonic Identifiers*

In creating identifiers, the programmer must guard against using identifiers whose relationships with their values is vague, tenuous, or peculiar to the programmer himself. The purpose of the following program segment has been obscured by the use of mnemonic identifiers and intermediate variables that appear reasonable at first glance but that are, in fact, misleading and confusing. State the purpose of this segment. What quantity is represented by "INTER"? Rewrite the segment using a better choice of mnemonic identifiers and intermediate variables

```
program TRICKYNAMES (INPUT, OUTPUT);
   var
      NUM, DENOM, SLOPE, INTER: REAL;
      ROW, COL:                INTEGER;
      A:                       array [1..2, 1..2] of REAL;

begin
   WRITE ('Enter values: ');
   for ROW := 1 to 2 do
      for COL := 1 to 2 do
         READ (A[ROW,COL]);

   if A[1,1] = A[2,1] then
      WRITELN ('NO VALUE')
   else
      begin
         NUM     := A[2,2] - A[1,2];
         DENOM   := A[2,1] - A[1,1];
         SLOPE   := NUM / DENOM;
         INTER   := A[1,2] - SLOPE * A[1,1];
         WRITELN := ('The answer is ', INTER)
      end
end.
```

| Exercise 2 | *Use of Psychologically "Distant" Identifiers* |

Consider the following program specification:

Input: three pairs of integers denoting the coordinates of three points on a grid.

Output: the area of the triangle defined by the three points.

Write such a program using *only* the identifiers X1, X2, X3, . . .

| Exercise 3 | *Global Variables* |

What is printed by the following piece of code?

```
program TROUBLES (INPUT, OUTPUT);
  var
    A: INTEGER;

function G(X: INTEGER): INTEGER;
begin
  A := 2 * (X + 1);
  G := A
end;

function F(X: INTEGER): INTEGER;
begin
  A := X + G(X);
  F := 2 * A
end;

begin
  A := 1;
  A := F(F(2)) + A;
  WRITELN (A)
end.
```

| Exercise 4 | *Disagreement* |

It is likely that you disagree strongly with at least one of the points raised in this chapter. Pick the one that you disagree with the most and prepare a comprehensive counterproposal. After the customary number of rewrites, have someone else read it. (Hint: Choose a friend to do the reading.)

Exercise 5   *An Essay*

Below are two advanced topics that we would have liked to discuss in this chapter. Pick the one that interests you the most, discuss the relevant issues, seek out the opinions of others, and present proposals which resolve some of the problems therein.

Topic 1: "The Problem with Problem Definitions"

Issues: How should one detail inputs and outputs? What constitutes a "complete" definition? How much of a definition can be used for documentation? Where do implementation requirements go? What about condition-action lists versus decision tables? How should the layout and organization of a good, complete definition appear?

Topic 2: "The Global Variable Problem"

Issues: Should Pascal limit the use of global variables? What changes would you make in Pascal to encourage better isolation of modules?

Exercise 6   *Mr. Croak*

There once was a frog named Mr. Croak, who was beset with three daughters of marriageable age, Ribbit1, Ribbit2, and Ribbit3. Now the only eligible male frog, Horatio, fell for Ribbit2 and proceeded to ask for her leg in marriage. However, Mr. Croak, concerned with the marriage prospects for Ribbit1 and Ribbit3, proposed the following: Whichever one of his daughters leaped the farthest would become Horatio's wife.

Now, Horatio knew, but Mr. Croak didn't, that Ribbit1 could jump three lily pads, that Ribbit2 could jump twice as far as Ribbit1, and that Ribbit3 could jump only one third as far as Ribbit2. Thus Horatio readily agreed and persuaded Mr. Croak that the following computer program should determine who would wed him. (Note: HEIGHTRIB1, HEIGHTRIB2, and HEIGHTRIB3 denote the heights of the jumps of Ribbits 1, 2, and 3.

What is the moral of the story?

```
program RIBBITS (INPUT, OUTPUT);
   var
       HEIGHTRIB1, HEIGHTRIB2, HEIGHTRIB3: REAL;

function F(var X: REAL): REAL;
begin
   X := 2 * X;
   F := X
end;

function G(var X: REAL): REAL;
begin
   X := (1/3) * X;
   G := X
end;

begin
   HEIGHTRIB1 := 3;
   HEIGHTRIB2 := F(HEIGHTRIB1);
   HEIGHTRIB3 := G(HEIGHTRIB2);

   WRITELN ('RIBBIT1 = ', HEIGHTRIB1,
            'RIBBIT2 = ', HEIGHTRIB2,
            'RIBBIT3 = ', HEIGHTRIB3)
end.
```

P A R T

THREE

THE PROVERBS IN ACTION

7 TOP-DOWN PROGRAMMING

❧

"THE PLAY'S THE THING."

Shakespeare
Hamlet, II, 2

A PROGRAMMER'S CHRISTMAS WORKSHOP

Act 1   *(The Problem)*

NARRATOR: This is not a fantasy or a play contrived solely for entertainment (although any applause will be graciously received). The play is about a problem and how it is defined, studied, and resolved using the top-down approach for programming. Implicitly and explicitly, the twenty-four proverbs for programming can be found operating in this little scenario. We hope the reader will be pleasantly surprised to see the proverbs in action. So, let the play begin!

Scene 1

[A corporate office. It is late afternoon in early May. Sam is sitting, staring at a blank but lighted terminal screen. The door opens. Walter enters.]

SAM: Walter . . . what news from the iron tower?

WALTER: Christmas is coming.

SAM: A four-hour meeting to tell me that?

WALTER: You may not make it home for the celebration.

SAM: *[Slumping deeper in his chair]* What is it this time?

WALTER: Samuel, I have been appointed to assign you the task of developing this year's most sought-after computer game: Kriegspiel Checkers!

SAM: *[Standing and wide-eyed]* WHATspiel checkers?!

WALTER: KRIEGspiel checkers! And just in time for Christmas!

Scene 2

[It is evening. Sam is home, slouched into a recliner chair in his den. He is reading from a pamphlet titled The International Rules and Conventions for Kriegspiel Checkers. *Tossing this aside, he begins to peruse the company's User Requirement Specification (the URS). He reads:]*

In Kriegspiel checkers, each player sits in an isolated area, having a separate board containing only his own pieces. Each move must follow the conventional rules for the game of checkers. However, as each player proposes a move, a third person, the referee (in this case, the computer program), tells the player that either

1. *the proposed move is legal, and the opponent will be directed to move;*

2. *the proposed move is illegal, and the player must propose another move; or*

3. *the proposed move wins and the game is over.*

Additional rules under the current Convention to the Rules are:

1. *A player may win the game by capturing or blocking all of the opponent's pieces, and he may also win by getting the first king.*

2. When a player proposes a legal jump that is part of a multiple jump, the referee informs the player that a further jump is required and the next square must be entered. The player then continues to propose moves to other squares until the multiple move is completed.

The program must "know" and enforce the rules of checkers, that is, ensure that black always moves first, insist that a jump be made when one is possible, verify the legality of moves, and determine when the game is over.

The rules of play are summarized as follows:

1. Black moves first.

2. Players take alternate moves: black then white, etc.

3. A player moves forward only, along diagonal paths.

4. A simple move is one square forward to an unoccupied square.

5. A jump move requires that an opponent's piece lie on the next forward square and that the square beyond is vacant.

6. If one or more jumps are possible for a player, then the move must be a jump move. If a jump can be continued to jump another piece, the jump must be continued.

7. When an opponent's piece is jumped, the opponent's piece is removed from the board. The piece is said to be "captured."

8. The game is won when a player either (1) captures all of the opponent's pieces, (2) places a piece on the opponent's back row (the king row), or (3) blocks all of the opponent's pieces so that none can move (a rare case).

The program must accept moves in a format familiar to the players. A move consists of two numbers corresponding to squares on a standard checkerboard. The first number denotes the square of the moving piece, and the second number is the destination square. The program must also output "messages" based on whether the proposed move is legal or not, requires a jump continuation, or terminates the game.

The program must be operational by September 1.

As an aid, the standard checkerboard numbering system is supplied with this URS.

Figure 46.   *Standard checkerboard numbering system*

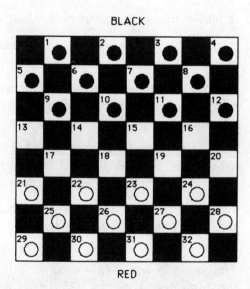

SAM: *[Thinking to himself]* Only Walter could have done this to me. And in ten weeks? Might as well call it Sam's Totenspiel. Looks like the perfect candidate for a top-down approach *[sighing]*—tomorrow.

Act II *(Program Specification)*

Scene 1

[The office. Three days later. It is morning. Walter enters, pours a cup of coffee, and sits down in a chair beside Sam's desk.]

SAM: Good morning, Walter. What's on your mind?

WALTER: The question is what's on yours—think you can handle the Kriegspiel?

SAM: Sure. But after looking over the marvelous International Rules and the URS, may I pass on some reflections of times past? *[Without waiting for an answer]* Remember that Daytona 500 Race game we did last spring?

WALTER: Who could forget it?

SAM: Right! And you know why we can't forget it? It was a lousy program. Why, you ask? Too many programming delays. And why, again, you ask? Lousy program analysis. We had a lot of time to get on with that program and we still didn't come off with anything sensational. But this time, we've only got eight weeks. And this time we're going to start from the top and work down.

WALTER: What do you propose?

SAM: *[He gets out of his chair and begins to walk in a circle around the desk.]* Walt, let's start by defining the problem better than we did last time. We need to get as complete a functional specification as we possibly can before we set one line of code.

WALTER: *[Picks up the telephone, dials]* Sally—hold my calls for a while.

SAM: *[Restlessly]* May I go on?

WALTER: Sam, I'm interested. You're my top programmer. What I think you're going to say is . . .

SAM: *[interrupting]* . . . is this. As simple as the inputs for Kriegspiel look on the surface, it's too easy to overlook some of the critical cases involved here. Let me review for a minute. The inputs are a series of pairs of numbers, right? *[Without waiting]* The first number represents the square designating a player's piece, and the second number represents the square to which that piece is to be moved. Of course, some of the pairs representing a move will result in a move that is illegal on a given board configuration.

WALTER: Go on.

SAM: Now suppose that a player inputs a number that doesn't correspond to a piece on the board. Why don't we sit down and make a list of such possibilities—we could call it our "error events list."

WALTER: Good idea. For example?

SAM: Easy. The player makes a simple typographical error—proposes a move that may contain characters that are not numbers at all or inputs a number that is too large to correspond with a numbered square on the board.

WALTER: Two more for the list.

SAM: If we keep the user in mind, we should ask ourselves right now: what kind of errors can they make in using this program? I think it's this kind of human engineering that we missed last time around. Let me ask you how we address these questions. What if the user inputs too many numbers? What if the user accidentally hits a carriage return and inputs no square number at all?

WALTER: Sam, why don't you do this for starters? Make out some kind of a table to spell out as carefully as you can all these kinds of input situations? *[Getting up]* I have to get ready for a budget meeting. I'd like to see what you come up with before we go much further.

SAM: Can do.

[Later that day, when Walter returns.]

174

Figure 47. **Format for input lines to Kriegspiel program**

Input field	Possible values	Error conditions
Normal move (2-squares)		
Leading string	Empty	None
First square number	$1 \leq$ integer ≤ 32	Number too large or too small; contains a non-numeric character
Separator string	A space or comma	Does not contain a space or comma
Second square number	$1 \leq$ integer ≤ 32	Number too large or too small; contains a non-numeric character
Trailing string	Any characters	None
Jump continuation move (1 square)		
Leading string	Empty	None
First square number	$1 \leq$ integer ≤ 32	Number too large or too small; contains a non-numeric character
Trailing string	Any characters	None

SAM: Behold, sire, I give you a table for Kriegspiel inputs and error messages.

WALTER: *[Looking at the paper. A pause.]* Sam, this is good stuff. I like this "trailing string" input.

SAM: Indeed. Gives the player the opportunity to annotate his game with running comments—after all, who knows when the classical Kriegspiel game is going to be played? Could be lost to all posterity.

WALTER: And now?

SAM: By tomorrow we should have the output messages specified.

WALTER: Any problems?

SAM: I don't think so. The outputs look like fairly simple messages printed to each player . . .

WALTER: *[interrupting]* . . . along with a display of the checkerboard with the players' pieces . . .

SAM: . . . right! But that's no problem. We'll pass the display problem over to Mary—for us, as Willie Shakespeare would say, "the play's the thing." *[Continuing as before]* There are a lot of possible messages, and I think we should get these in concrete now, rather than coming up with some new innovative message halfway downstream after we start coding. Most of these message requirements are already written into the URS.

WALTER: Sam: some guidelines. These messages have to be short because they're going to be repetitive. And I think that the messages should give the user specific information, especially in those cases where the user makes an error.

SAM: I agree. I should have the proposed output messages for your approval in the morning.

Scene 2

[The office again, two days later. Sam and Walter have been reviewing the first product of Sam's efforts: the proposed output messages and a sample screen layout from Janet's desk.]

SAM: Walt, this took a little longer than I thought. But I thought I should also make a sketch of the input situations to the output responses for Kriegspiel. This gives the programmers who ultimately develop the program the conditions that describe the actions and output response to each action. *[He hands Walter another paper.]*

Figure 48. *Output messages for Kriegspiel program*

```
Introductory message for player with black pieces
WELCOME TO KRIEGSPIEL CHECKERS.
MOVES ARE GIVEN AS TWO SQUARE NUMBERS, FOR INSTANCE, 9 14

Introductory message for player with red pieces
WELCOME TO KRIEGSPIEL CHECKERS.
MOVES ARE GIVEN AS TWO SQUARE NUMBERS, FOR INSTANCE, 21 17
YOUR OPPONENT WILL MAKE THE FIRST MOVE.

Prompt player for a normal (2-square) move
IT IS YOUR TURN TO MOVE:

Prompt player for a (1-square) jump continuation
YOUR JUMP MUST BE CONTINUED.
ENTER JUMP SQUARE ONLY:

Acknowledge legal move
OK, YOUR OPPONENT HAS BEEN ASKED TO MOVE.

Non-numeric characters in input square
NON-NUMERIC CHARACTERS IN SQUARE NUMBER.
TRY AGAIN:

Illegal square number
SQUARE NUMBER OUT OF RANGE 1 TO 32.
TRY AGAIN:

No space or comma between square numbers
NO SPACE OR COMMA BETWEEN SQUARE NUMBERS.
TRY AGAIN:

Jump exists and has not been taken
A JUMP IS AVAILABLE AND YOU MUST TAKE IT.
TRY AGAIN:

Illegal move
TRY AGAIN:

Illegal jump continuation
ILLEGAL JUMP CONTINUATION.
TRY AGAIN:
```

```
Piece captured
PIECE CAPTURED.

Losing message
SORRY. . .YOUR OPPONENT HAS WON THE GAME!!!

Winning message
CONGRATULATIONS. . .YOU HAVE WON THE GAME!!!
```

Figure 49.   *Sample screen layout*

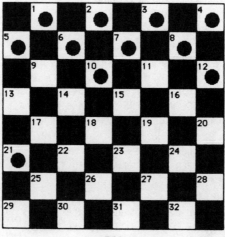

IT'S YOUR TURN TO MOVE: 10 45

SQUARE NUMBER OUT OF RANGE 1 TO 32

TRY AGAIN: 10 15

Figure 50. *Mapping of input situations to output responses*

Print introductory message to each player, and prompt black player for a normal (2-square) move.

CONDITION	ACTION
1 Game has not been won and a normal (2-square) move is required.	Prompt player for a normal (2-square) move.
1.1 First or second field of input line is not a number.	Print message indicating illegal characters.
1.2 First or second field is a number that is not a legal square number.	Print message indicating square number out range.
1.3 Separator is not a blank or comma.	Print message indicating illegal separator.
1.4 First and second fields are legal square numbers.	
1.4.1 Move is illegal on the current board configuration.	Print message indicating illegal move.
1.4.2 Move is a legal non-jump but a jump exists.	Print message that a jump must be taken.
1.4.3 Move is a legal non-jump and no jump exists.	Print message indicating a completed legal move, process the move, and prompt the opponent.
1.4.4 Move is a legal jump and does not require a continuation.	Print message indicating that a piece was captured and that a legal move has been completed, process the move, and prompt the opponent.
1.4.5 Move is a legal jump and requires a continuation.	Print message indicating that a piece was captured, and process a jump continuation.
2 Game has not been won and a jump continuation (1-square) move is required.	Prompt player for a jump continuation (1-square) move.

2.1 The jump square field is not a number.	Print message indicating illegal characters.
2.2 The jump square field is not a legal square number.	Print message indicating square out of range.
2.3 The jump continuation contiuation.	Print message for illegal jump continuation.
2.4 The jump continuation square is legal.	Print message acknowledging legal continuation and process move.
3 Game has been won.	Print winning and losing messages.

WALTER: *[After reading and comparing the three documents]* Sam, you know what you've done here? *[Without waiting for an answer]* You, sir, have completed the functional specification for user requirements. I simply can't recall if we've ever done it this way before, surely not with the Daytona 500 project. And as such, I say that this is a milestone, almost, in our software development process. What do you say to that?

SAM: Would you repeat that to the payroll officer?

WALTER: Very funny. *[Rhetorically]* What next? Before you translate an answer into a pay raise, let me tell you. Documentation. Gather all this stuff together and make a draft for the programmer's documentation manual. Copies to me, members of the operations board, and probably most important, to a few of your colleagues down here. Get their reviews as soon as you can. Remember how we're going about this project . . .

SAM: *[Interrupting]* . . . yes, I know. "Top-down development does not proceed until all the criticism is in."

WALTER: Sam, you've got a good start. You haven't panicked. You've questioned and defined the problem and the documentation will be done as soon as you review the responses you get. You're thinking *now*. That's good. You can code later. Don't break this top-down approach pattern, Sam. There's always a temptation to hark back to those other approaches that got us in trouble before. Let's not do it this time.

SAM: Right. I think we're off to a good start.

Act III   *(Top-Down Programming)*

Scene 1

[Walter's office. He answers the intercom.]

VOICE: *[Sally's.]* She's here.

WALTER: Please have her come in. *[Walter goes to the door. It opens before he reaches it.]* Janet! How good to see you again! Please sit down. Coffee?

JANET: Thank you. I hope I'm not late.

WALTER: On the contrary. we weren't expecting you until Monday. *[Pouring the coffee]* All finished now in academia?

JANET: *[With a sigh]* At last! *[Pausing]* And now . . . ?

WALTER: You could not have come at a better time. You didn't meet Sam during your interviews. But you'll be working with him on a new project—Kriegspiel Checkers—has to be done in seven weeks. We've had the URS in hand for a week and Sam's just about finished with the specification. I think, rather than reviewing the status myself right now, as seeing as it's Friday afternoon, why don't I send you on down and Sam can fill you in on the progress. *[Going to the desk, dialing the intercom.]* Sam, Janet is here—I told you help was on the way. Seems like a good time for a briefing on the Kriegspiel before the weekend.

SAM: Good. We'll be all ready for next week.

WALTER: *[Hanging up the phone]* Well, Janet, Sam will be waiting for you. *[In a more serious tone.]* Janet, we have a new challenge here. Sam is an old-time programmer who has been through a lot of programs—some good, some not so good. You'll be working in a different way than you might have learned in college. We think we are going to solve a lot of problems around here with the "top-down" approach—it's really nothing new, just getting back to some basics. Sam has got it rolling now, and you'll have the chance to be on the ground floor of our first effort to bring this approach back to our programming. In many ways, maybe you can lend some new ideas to this effort. Good luck, young lady. *[He shows her to the door.]*

Scene 2

[Sam is alone in the room, seated with his back to the door and does not see Janet come in. She closes the door.]

JANET: Hello, I'm Janet.

SAM: *[Turning in his chair, standing.]* Welcome! I'm more than delighted! I learned a long time ago that sometimes a woman's view of a programming problem has more merit to it than most of us men admit. Mary, who does most of our presentation work, has a knack for it that none of the men, including me, have ever been able to apply to some of the problems. *[Pausing].* So, you're just out of school?

JANET: Yes. *[She looks at paper-strewn desk]* And speaking of that, I was trained to keep things as short and simple as possible. This hardly looks like . . .

SAM: Don't let the appearance overwhelm you. You may have been taught correctly. But the complexity lies in the problem itself—we can't avoid that, especially with this Kriegspiel. It is we programmers who are tasked with reducing complexity to manageable simplicity. Let me show you.

[He spends an hour with Janet going over the URS, the princi-
ples of the top-down approach, and the work that he has done
so far]

SAM: . . . so there you have a brief idea of what the problem is all
about and how it should work with this program. What we
hope happens here is that now that the specification of the
problem has been completed, we won't have to make any programming changes during development or coding. O.K. so far?

JANET: Sounds good. What do you want me to do?

SAM: Well, there's not much we can do at 4 o'clock on a Friday afternoon. But I've just finished the functional specifications and
I want you to start on the top-down development of the program next week. Why don't you take this with you over the
weekend. Monday's my monthly "meeting" day and I won't be
here to bother you—that will give you time to see what you
can do to get started. The desk over there is yours. *[Pausing as*
he begins gathering his papers.] I hope you can lock into this
top-down approach as quickly as possible. Remember some of
these ideas are relatively new for me, too. And for Walter.
Someday when this is all over, remind me to tell you about the
Daytona 500 race.

Scene 3

[Tuesday morning. Janet is at her desk when Sam arrives.]

SAM: Well, the early bird! And coffee made already! *[He unpacks his*
briefcase.]

JANET: I've made a first pass at the program, Sam.

SAM: Let me fill my cup and have a look. *[With his coffee, he exam-*
ines the paper.]

```
P1 (first pass)

initialize program variables
welcome players
```

```
repeat
    get a proposed move
    if move is legal
        then process the move
    if the game is not over
        then change players
    else exit
until game over

end the game and stop
```

SAM: Not bad, in fact, I'm delighted for the second day on the job. Shows some imagination. But . . .

JANET: *[Interrupting]* . . . here it comes.

SAM: *[Quickly.]* No, the first thing around here you'll find is that criticism is not directed toward any one person—criticism is for improvement. Later I'll show all the comments I got when I sent the functional specification around last week. But in almost every case, the critics had something to contribute, and they solved a lot of problems we might have found later—and much to our later regret. So let's take a look at this first pass. *[They sit down together at his desk.]*

SAM: If you have any questions as we go through this, stop so we can both know what the answers are. *[Pausing.]* Three things are apparent. First, you mention the initialization of some program variables but you don't specify which variables are to be initialized and which messages are to be printed. Second, no mention is made of whether a legal move is in fact a part of a jump situation in which the player must input a square to continue the jump. This notation "process the move" is a nebulous subroutine—we'll have to formalize it somewhat. And, third, as you'll find out in the top-down approach, we discard any exits and goto's—nay, all exits and goto's in the program. These clutter a program—maybe not for us—but for the somebody else that is going to read this program someday. So let's see what you and I together can do with a second pass at this.

[In a surprisingly short time, they develop this:]

```
P1 (second pass)

initialize (PLAYER, BOARD)
write (INTRODUCTORY_MESSAGES)

repeat
    get (MOVE) from PLAYER
    if LEGAL_MOVE (PLAYER, BOARD, MOVE) then
        UPDATE_BOARD (PLAYER, BOARD, MOVE)

        if LEGAL_JUMP (PLAYER, BOARD, MOVE)
        and JUMP_CAN_BE_CONTINUED (PLAYER, BOARD, MOVE) then
            CONTINUE_THE_JUMP (PLAYER, BOARD, MOVE)

        if NO_KING (BOARD, PLAYER)
        and MOVES_LEFT (BOARD, OPPONENT) then
            swap PLAYERS
            prompt OPPONENT for NEXT MOVE
        else
            write (WINNING_MSG) for PLAYER
            write (LOSING_MSG) for OPPONENT
            GAME_OVER is true
    else
            write (ILLEGAL_MOVE_MSG) for PLAYER
until GAME_OVER
```

SAM: What do you think about this one?

JANET: You first.

SAM: O.K. For one thing, this version calls for one subroutine to check for a legal move and a later subroutine to check if the legal move was a jump and that the jump can be continued. What are we doing with two subroutines? The check for a legal move includes a check for a jump that may need to be continued if it is part of a multiple jump. So why recompute this frequently executed test after it has already been determined to be legal? Why don't we have a single subroutine to check for the legality of the move and return two flags: one that indicates whether the move was legal and the other indicating whether the jump must be continued?

JANET: And?

SAM: And that's not enough. If the move is not legal, one of several messages must be issued. These depend on the kind of error made. I would think that a good way to deal with this situation is to enumerate all possible outcomes. In particular use this: *[He writes:]*

```
type
    MOVE_STATUS_VALUE =
        (ILLEGAL_SQ_NUM, SQ_OUT_OF_RANGE, ILLEGAL_SEPARATOR,
        ILLEGAL_MOVE, JUMP_EXISTS, MOVE_OK,
        JUMP_COMPLETED, JUMP_CONTINUATION
```

Now the evaluation of a move can return the appropriate status value. A case statement can then be used to take the appropriate action.

JANET: Sam, something about the clarity and, to overuse the word, efficiency of the program bothers me. Look here. Passing BOARD as a parameter to almost every function and subroutine seems inefficient. The general use of the BOARD variable is obvious and shouldn't it be passed as an explicit argument to each function and subroutine?

SAM: No, and I'll tell you why. I've heard this argument before and maybe when the program is finished, we can argue about it later. But we want to black-box these subroutines. Although it seems obvious, it's not very efficient. What you're talking about, of course, is global variables, and I don't think you have a case for clarity, either. Spelling out the design in complete detail is what counts now, especially now as we start coding. In the long run, global variables destroy clarity.

JANET: Sam. A question. You've been talking about thinking first—coding later, black-boxing subroutines, the top-down approach: is all this something new?

SAM: New? It's been around for twenty years. Walter was in here last week looking at what has to be done. He's been around a long time and what he had to say was simply a review of the top-down approach. *[He mellows.]* It's just that we've been so caught up in getting a program coded that we haven't been paying attention to the basics of programming. We forget the user. We stop reading the literature. And we wonder why programs crash two days before the deadline. But if we carry on as we are now, Kriegspiel won't crash. *[Looking again at the paper.]* For instance, we still have a small error in our second pass.

JANET: Oh?

SAM: See here? The variable OPPONENT occurs in the code but has not been given a value. Obviously, the OPPONENT is the other PLAYER. In addition, GAME–OVER has not been initialized. These points have to be spelled out. Listen: we can postpone some of these decisions for the time being about data representations for the board and players. Some of these decisions are usually limiting anyway, since there is a tendency to program around the properties of the representations.

JANET: Shall we try again?

SAM: Why not?

[They are busy once more and produce the third pass.]

```
P1 (third pass)


SET_UP (BOARD)
PLAYER := BLACK
OPPONENT := RED



write (BLACK_INTRO_MSG)
write (RED_INTRO_MSG)
GAME_OVER := FALSE



repeat
    get (MOVE) from PLAYER
    EVALUATE_MOVE using BOARD, PLAYER, MOVE giving MOVE_STATUS
```

```
case MOVE_STATUS of
    ILLEGAL_SQ_NUM, SQ_OUT_OF_RANGE, ILLEGAL_SEPARATOR,
    ILLEGAL_MOVE, JUMP_EXISTS =>
        WRITE_STATUS_MSG (MOVE_STATUS) for PLAYER

    MOVE_OK, JUMP_COMPLETED =>
        UPDATE_BOARD using BOARD, PLAYER, MOVE
        if GAME_WON (BOARD, PLAYER) then
            GAME_OVER := TRUE
        else
            WRITE_STATUS_MSG (MOVE_STATUS) for PLAYER
            PROMPT_NEW_MOVE for OPPONENT
            SWAP (PLAYER, OPPONENT)

    JUMP_CONTINUATION =>
        WRITE_STATUS_MSG (MOVE_STATUS) for PLAYER
        CONTINUE_THE_JUMP using PLAYER updating BOARD

    end
until GAME_OVER

write (WINNING_MSG) for PLAYER
write (LOSING_MSG) for PLAYER
```

SAM: Now, dear lady, what do you think?

JANET: I think we've got it!

SAM: Maybe. But let's give it a rest. See you in the morning.

Scene 4

[The office again, next day.]

SAM: *[Looking at Janet as he toys with the spoon in his coffee cup.]* Something bothering you this morning?

JANET: It came to me last night—and has been nagging me ever since. It's in this top-level design (the CONTINUE_THE_JUMP). It doesn't make sense. Like the main program loop, it will have to prompt the player, evaluate moves, and issue diagnostics. It may even lead to a winning move, yet we haven't taken these possibilities into account.

SAM: I see what you mean.

JANET: We're trying to handle these matters in a subroutine and that is just like writing the main loop again! And what about updating the BOARD again?

SAM: You are saying we have a problem?

JANET: *[Somewhat disconcerted.]* I'm not sure. But I'm afraid now that the way we are handling error messages is not going to work. When we're getting moves, we can find errors in the format. And when we're evaluating moves, we find erroneous play. Can these really be handled together?

SAM: Back to the drawing board? Don't be afraid to start over. Let's see what the next pass will yield.

[After a few hours, Sam and Janet are satisfied at last.]

```
Pl (fourth pass)

SET_UP (BOARD)
PLAYER := BLACK
OPPONENT := RED
write (BLACK_INTRO_MSG) for PLAYER
write (RED_INTRO_MSG)   for OPPONENT

GAME_OVER := FALSE
JUMP_AGAIN := FALSE
repeat
   if JUMP_AGAIN then
      GET_SINGLE_SQ_MOVE from PLAYER using CONTINUE_SQ
                         giving MOVE
   else
      GET_TWO_SQ_MOVE from PLAYER giving MOVE
   EVALUATE_MOVE using BOARD, PLAYER, MOVE giving MOVE_STATUS

   case MOVE_STATUS of
      JUMP_EXISTS =>
         WRITE_STATUS_MSG (JUMP_EXISTS_MSG)

      ILLEGAL_MOVE =>
         if JUMP_AGAIN then
            WRITE_STATUS_MSG (JUMP_CONT) for PLAYER
         else
            WRITE_STATUS_MSG (ILLEGAL_MOVE) for PLAYER
```

```
        MOVE_OK, JUMP_COMPLETED =>
            UPDATE_BOARD using PLAYER, MOVE updating BOARD
            if GAME_WON (BOARD, PLAYER) then
                GAME_OVER := TRUE
            else
                WRITE_STATUS_MSG (MOVE_OK) for PLAYER
                PROMPT_NEW_MOVE for OPPONENT
                SWAP (PLAYER, OPPONENT)
                JUMP_AGAIN := FALSE

        JUMP_CONTINUATION =>
            UPDATE_BOARD using PLAYER, MOVE updating BOARD
            JUMP_AGAIN := TRUE
            CONTINUE_SQ := SECOND_SQ(MOVE)

    until GAME_OVER

    write (WINNING_MSG) for PLAYER
    write (LOSING_MSG)  for OPPONENT
```

SAM: Just when you thought you had it, you have to do it again.

JANET: All right, but what's so wrong about starting over?

SAM: *[To himself.]* You're learning, I'm learning.

Act IV *(Data Representation)*

Scene 1

[The office. The next day. Janet and Sam are having coffee, looking at the standard checkerboard.]

SAM: Janet, now that we've settled on our algorithm, we have to determine what is called "the specific structure of the data representations." All this means is that we have to figure out a way to represent the checkerboard and the player's pieces in the program. It's tempting to code this standard checkerboard numbering system into the program, but the problem is more difficult than it first appears.

JANET: How so?

SAM: First, look at square 10. A black piece on that square can make a nonjump move to squares 14 or 15. So the possible moves are $(10 + 4) = 14$, or $(10 + 5) = 15$, or simply $+4$, $+5$. But from square 15 the black moves are to squares 18 or 19, or simply $+3$, $+4$. A similar situation exists for red, except that the moves are -3, -4, and -4, -5, since the move direction is reversed. Now we could sort out which moves use the 3,4 rule and which moves use the 4,5 rule, but we have another problem. Black's first row (squares 1 through 4) uses the $+4, +5$ rule. But what about square 4? Using the $+4, +5$ rules, square 8 is a legal square but square 9 is not.

JANET: Sam, maybe I have a solution. I was thinking about just what you have said and I brought in this old article from the *Scientific American. [See Strachey, 1971]*

SAM: Enlighten me, if you will.

JANET: In this scheme, regardless of the square, the possible directed moves for black are always $+4$ and $+5$, and -4 and -5 for red. The added border squares are "flag" squares. They contain some value to indicate that they do not represent legal squares. If a proposed move goes from a legal square to a "flag" square, the move will be detected as illegal. The opposite border squares are labeled with the same numbers. This doesn't cause any confusion because they are flag squares and as such will always appear as illegal moves.

SAM: *[After some thought.]* Yes, Janet, this solves a lot of problems. But you know: the players use the standard checkerboard, and the program will have to use this one. This inconsistency means that the input moves will have to be converted to Samuels' representation. This could be tricky.

[Walter enters.]

WALTER: Well, you two seem to be hard at it. A progress report?

Figure 51. *Alternative numbering for internal representation of a checkerboard*

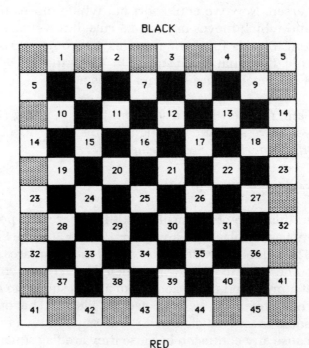

BLACK

RED

SAM: We have settled on the algorithm and we are coming to grips on the board representation. But we don't . . .

JANET: What Sam is trying to say, Walter, is that we need to do some thinking about this before we go on.

WALTER: O.K., but I'm looking forward to a prototype system pretty soon. May I remind you of how many shopping days there are until Christmas?

SAM: Walt, we're close. With a few days for incubation, I think we'll find a solution.

Scene 2

[The office, three days later. Janet is at her desk when Sam arrives.]

JANET: Sam, get your coffee and listen to an idea that I have.

SAM: *[He pours a cup, and settles into his chair.]* Do proceed.

JANET: Sam, I've done a lot of thinking for the past few days. It's the board that's giving us a problem, right?

SAM: Right.

JANET: If we think about the board, we should realize that the board has two distinct uses. First, it is a record of the current status of the game. Second, it is a means for determining the legal squares for proposed moves. Aside from the pieces on the actual board, the possible legal squares for a player's moves are constant. Constant, Sam! Why not let the legal square from each square be stored in a constant array? For example—and using the standard checkerboard—for a black piece on square 14, the only possible nonjumps are to squares 17 and 18, and the only possible jumps are to squares 21 and 23. As for the current status of the game, we can maintain a separate array to keep track of the current board configuration.

SAM: I follow all this.

JANET: I drew up this table, Sam. There are some left and right moves that have no legal square, but this won't be a problem because we can always make a special value for this case. For the current status of the board, we can represent the conventional, that is, the 32-square board layout in the form of a 32-element array.

Figure 52. *Table of adjacent squares. Dashes represent illegal moves*

Square	Left adjacent square	Right adjacent square	Left jump square	Right square
BLACK				
1	5	6	—	10
2	6	7	9	11
3	7	8	10	12
4	8	—	11	—
5	—	9	—	14
.	.	.	.	.
.	.	.	.	.
.	.	.	.	.
31	—	—	—	—
32	—	—	—	—
RED				
1	—	—	—	—
2	—	—	—	—
.	.	.	.	.
.	.	.	.	.
.	.	.	.	.
28	24	—	19	—
29	—	25	—	22
30	25	26	21	23
31	26	27	22	24
32	27	28	23	—

SAM: Janet, you've done it! This is the transition we needed. Now let's see—although this appears easy, there are all kinds of representations for it. With: *[He pauses for a minute then writes on the blackboard:]*

```
type
    COLOR       = (BLACK, RED);
    DIRECTION   = (LEFT_ADJ, LEFT_JUMP, RIGHT_ADJ, RIGHT_JUMP);
    DESTINATION = 0..32;   { -- 0 denotes an empty space }
```

We could have:

a. *One large two-dimensional array*

```
type
    LEGAL_ADJ_SQ = array [1..64, DIRECTION] of DESTINATION;
```

b. *One large three-dimensional array*

```
type
    LEGAL_ADJ_SQ = array [COLOR, 1..32, DIRECTION]
                        of DESTINATION;
```

c. *Two two-dimensional arrays*

```
type
    LEGAL_ADJ_SQ = array [1..32, DIRECTION]
                        of DESTINATION;
var
    RED_ADJ_SQ,
    BLACK_ADJ_SQ: LEGAL_ADJ_SQ;
```

d. *Eight one-dimensional arrays*

```
type
    LEGAL_MOVE = array [1..32] of DESTINATION;

var
    BLACK_LEFT, BLACK_LEFT_JUMP,
    BLACK_RIGHT, BLACK_RIGHT_JUMP,
    RED_LEFT, RED_LEFT_JUMP,
    RED_RIGHT, RED_RIGHT_JUMP: LEGAL_MOVE;
```

e. *A record structure for the possible adjacent squares*

```
type
    ADJ_SQ =
            record
                LEFT_ADJ:    DESTINATION;
                LEFT_JUMP:   DESTINATION;
                RIGHT_JUMP:  DESTINATION;
                LEFT_JUMP:   DESTINATION
            end;
```

JANET: *[After she and Sam have discussed the options at some length.]*
I think option (a) is confusing and should be rejected.

SAM: I agree. And I think it's time for lunch.

[In the afternoon, they return.]

JANET: Sam—that cafeteria of yours—remind me to bring my lunch tomorrow. *[Returning to the blackboard again.]* It seems in part that the issue depends on whether the PLAYER and the move option (LEFT_ADJ, LEFT_JUMP, RIGHT_ADJ, RIGHT_JUMP) need to be thought of as variables. *[She goes to the blackboard.]* For instance, with an array A of legal adjacent squares and

```
PLAYER := RED
MOVE   := LEFT_JUMP
```

one cannot say things like:

```
A_MOVE[SQ]    { -- meaning RED_LEFT_JUMP[SQ] }
A.MOVE[SQ]    { -- meaning RED.LEFT_JUMP[SQ] }
```

This essentially rules out (d) and (e). It seems reasonable, also, to use a COLOR as an array index. This seems to leave us (b) or (c). But wait, how about a variant of these two choices:

```
type
    ADJACENT_SQS = array [COLOR, 1..32] of DESTINATION
var
    LEFTADJ_SQ, LEFT_JUMP_SQ,
    RIGHT_ADJ_SQ, RIGHT_JUMP_SQ: ADJACENT_SQS;
```

SAM: There seems to be no doubt.

JANET: Agreed? Now all we have to do is to summarize this in written form.

[They spend the rest of the day working together; this is the product:]

```
type
    COLOR:     (BLACK,RED);
    SQ_STATUS: (BLACK_PIECE, RED_PIECE, VACANT);

    INPUT_STATUS_VALUE =
        (ILLEGAL_SQ,    NO_SEPARATOR,  SQUARE_OUT_OF_RANGE,
         ILLEGAL_MOVE,  MOVE_OK,       JUMP_EXISTS,
         JUMP,          JUMP_CONT);
```

```
MSG_NAME =
    (ILLEGAL_SQ_MSQ,   NO_SEPARATOR_MSG, SQ_OUT_OF_RANGE_MSG,
     ILLEGAL_MOVE_MSG, JUMP_EXISTS_MSG,  JUMP_CONT_MSG, PIECE_TAKEN_MSG,
     BLACK_INTRO_MSG,  RED_INTO_MSG,     WINNING_MSG,   LOSING_MSG);

SQ_VALUE     = 1..32;
DESTINATION  = 0..32;   { -- no destination is denoted by 0 }
MOVE_PAIR    =
    record
        SQ1: SQ_VALUE;
        SQ2: SQ_VALUE
    end;

BOARD_CONTENTS = array [1..32] of SQ_STATUS;
ADJACENT_SQS   = array [COLOR, 1..32] of DESTINATION;

var
    BLACKSTERMINAL, REDSTERMINAL: TEXT;
    PLAYER, OPPONENT: COLOR;

    BOARD: BOARDCONTENTS;

    LEFTADJSQ,  LEFTJUMPSQ,
    RIGHTADJSQ, RIGHTJUMPSQ: ADJACENTSQS;

    MOVE:       MOVEPAIR;
    MOVESTATUS: INPUTSTATUS;

    CONTINUESQ: SQVALUE;
    GAMEOVER,
    JUMPAGAIN:  BOOLEAN;
```

SAM: Janet, may I give us each a compliment? I think we've jolly-well resolved this problem. I think we're ready to start writing the main program and—you know what?—I think it's going to be easy.

Scene 3

NARRATOR: The scene returns to the office, a week later. All the while, Janet has been piecing the main program together. The result of her efforts is shown at the end of the play as Figure 53. Let us return to the action!

SAM: *[Seeing what Janet has done.]* Janet, you must forgive my curiosity. I'll have more time to read all this later. But it seems to me that things have been going so well so far, I wonder if you would show me one subprogram—to sort of see if the proof is really in the pudding.

JANET: Why not? Here's the one that was most difficult: EVALUATEMOVE. This subroutine takes three input arguments: BOARD, PLAYER, MOVE. It returns a value for the MOVESTATUS indicator. For a legal move, the following conditions must be met:

— *SQ1 and SQ2 are the part of a MOVE.*

1. *The moving player must have a piece on SQ1.*

2. *SQ2 must be vacant.*

3. *SQ2 must be a left or right adjacent square.*

4. *If the move is a jump, the intervening square must contain an opponent's piece and SQ2 must be an adjacent jump square.*

5. *If a jump exists for the moving player, the move must be a jump.*

The legal adjacent squares are determined by the constant arrays LEFTADJSQ, RIGHTADJSQ, LEFTJUMPSQ, and RIGHTJUMPSQ. The function JUMPAVAILABLE determines whether a player has a jump.

SAM: Janet, I think we've both learned something. Using the top-down approach, we've been able to define and structure all the procedures so carefully that all of the procedures, as you've just demonstrated here, can be written independently. All the other subprograms will fit the required definitions of the main program.

JANET: So now, Sam, will you tell me about Daytona 500?

SAM: I promise you, you don't want to know.

CURTAIN

NARRATOR: This play, with any suitable change of names and places, is by and large an accurate portrayal of reality. Throughout the play, the top-down approach was, indeed, followed. In all fairness, let us summarize what actually happened.

First, the inputs, outputs, and condition-action mapping underwent many revisions as Sam and Janet wrote the actual program. It would be nice to think that an ideal situation would be that this kind of revision is unnecessary, but it seldom happens.

Second, it was important to alter the move status values and to alter the error diagnostics. In lower-level modules, there were several detailed problems. We consider these as flaws. On programming issues, name changes were made which even affected the main program.

Finally, there were debates on the actual kind of error checking performed by the program. This is a difficult issue to address, and the influence of Pascal had some effect on our final compromise. We believe, however, that the lessons demonstrated in this play are applicable to programming in general, regardless of the language being employed.

This play demonstrates, as do the proverbs, the value of the top-down approach. The overall effect of this little scenario is, I think, to emphasize the importance of thinking, and especially, thinking before any code is written.

For your information, the final program is included in this book as Appendix B.

Figure 53.   *Final pass at the main program*

```
INITIALIZE (BOARD);
SETUPBLACK (LEFTADJSQ, LEFTJUMPSQ, RIGHTADJSQ, RIGHTJUMPSQ);
SETUPRED   (LEFTADJSQ, LEFTJUMPSQ, RIGHTADJSQ, RIGHTJUMPSQ);
PLAYER   := BLACK;
OPPONENT := RED;
```

```
      SENDMSG (OPPONENT, REDINTROMSG);
      SENDMSG (PLAYER,   BLACKINTROMSG);
      SENDMSG (PLAYER,   NEWMOVEMSG);

      GAMEOVER  := FALSE;
      JUMPAGAIN := FALSE;
      repeat
         if JUMPAGAIN then
            GETONESQMOVE ({using} PLAYER, CONTINUESQ, {giving}  MOVE)
         else
            GETTWOSQMOVE ({using} PLAYER, {giving} MOVE);

         EVALUATEMOVE ({using} PLAYER, MOVE, BOARD, {giving} MOVESTATUS);
         case MOVESTATUS of
            JUMPEXISTS: SENDMSG (PLAYER, JUMPEXISTSMSG);
            ILLEGALMOVE: if JUMPAGAIN then
                            SENDMSG (PLAYER, JUMPCONTMSG)
                         else
                            SENDMSG (PLAYER, ILLEGALMOVEMSG);
            MOVEOK,
            JUMP:        begin
                            UPDATEBOARD (PLAYER, MOVE, BOARD);
                            if MOVESTATUS = JUMP then
                               SENDMSG (PLAYER, PIECETAKENMSG);
                            if GAMEWON (PLAYER, BOARD) then
                               GAMEOVER := TRUE
                            else
                               begin
                                  SENDMSG (PLAYER, MOVEOKMSG);
                                  SENDMSG (OPPONENT, NEWMOVEMSG);
                                  SWAP (PLAYER,  OPPONENT);
                                  JUMPAGAIN := FALSE
                               end
                         end;
            JUMPCONT:    begin
                            UPDATEBOARD (PLAYER, MOVE, BOARD);
                            SENDMSG (PIECETAKENMSG);
                            SENDMSG (PLAYER, JUMPCONTMSG);
                            JUMPAGAIN := TRUE;
                            CONTINUESQ := MOVE.SQ2
                         end
         end
      until GAMEOVER;

      SENDMSG (PLAYER,   WINNINGMSG);
      SENDMSG (OPPONENT, LOSINGMSG)
```

TOP-DOWN PROGRAMMING REVISITED

This chapter presents a technique of program development generally known as top-down programming. The top-down approach presented here is based on the notions of "structured programming" [see Dahl et. al., 1972] and "stepwise refinement" [Wirth, 1971]. While the technique is not a panacea for all programming ills, it does offer strong guidelines for an intelligent approach to a programming problem.

Before coding, every programmer must have in hand a complete statement of the problem, a well-planned documentation system, and a clear design strategy. The input format, legal and illegal fields, output files, reports, program messages, and the mapping from all various input data situations to their correct outputs must be described in detail. Furthermore, the overall algorithm must also be determined before coding. It is senseless to start coding a program without such a complete attack on the problem. The top-down approach has the following characteristics:

1. Design in levels. *The programmer designs the program in levels, where a level consists of one or more modules. A module is always "complete," although it may reference unwritten submodules. The first level is a complete "main program." A lower level refines or develops unwritten modules in the upper level. The programmer may look several levels ahead to determine the best way to design the level at hand.*

2. Initial language independence. *The programmer initially uses expressions (often in English or pseudo-code) that are relevant to the problem solution, even though the expressions cannot be directly transliterated into code. From statements that are machine and language independent, the programmer moves toward a final implementation in a programming language.*

3. Postponement of details to lower levels. *The programmer concentrates on critical broad issues at the initial levels and postpones details (for example, choice of specific algorithms or intermediate data representations) until lower levels.*

4. Formalization of each level. *Before proceeding to a lower level, the programmer ensures that the "program" in its current stage of development is a "formal" statement. In most cases, this means a program that calls unwritten submodules with all arguments spelled out. This step ensures that further sections of the program will be developed independently, without having to change the specifications or the interface bettween modules.*

5. Verification of each level. *After generating the modules of a new level, the programmer verifies the developing formal statement of the program.*

6. Successive refinements. *Each level of the program is refined, formalized, and verified successively until the programmer obtains a completed program that can be transformed easily into code.*

One should note several things about the top-down approach. First, the entire problem and its overall solution are presumed to be understood. It is senseless to start programming until there is a complete understanding of the problem and a complete general plan of attack. Such an understanding allows the programmer to write the program without losing sight of the overall goal.

Second, at the upper levels, the approach is machine and language independent. The programmer is not constrained by the details of a programming language. He or she is writing the upper levels using a notation that meaningfully solves the problem, although it might not be understood by a language processor. The programmer's use of a particular notation involves no sacrifice. At each level the statements produced still represent a complete program in some sense. All that is lacking is the machine capable of executing the statement.

Third, at each level of design, informal notation must be formalized as a hypothetical, but explicitly specified, procedure. Specification involves a complete listing of all input and output arguments.

Fourth, at each level the programmer must verify the program in its present form so that further refinements will be absolutely correct with respect to previously designed levels. This usually means running and testing the code already written. The unwritten modules needed for the code are filled in some temporary way. Such dummy modules are called "stubs."

For example, suppose that a programmer is working at an intermediate level and generates the following informal statement:

```
case day-of-the-week of

    Monday:      generate last week's data summary
    Tuesday:     do nothing
    Wednesday:   update usage file
    Thursday:    process new data
    Friday:      generate lab item reports
    Saturday:    generate weekly breakage statistics
    Sunday:      do nothing


end
```

The language of this statement is far removed from a programming language. On the other hand, the statement is perfectly clear to the programmer in that it reflects a portion of the desired code. The programmer must elaborate on the required inputs and expected outputs for the procedures like "generate lab item reports" and "update usage file." The next levels of refinement must develop each procedure.

The process of solving a problem using the top-down approach is a matter of successive refinements. The topmost level represents the general conception of the problem. At each successive level, the alternative design decisions are exposed. The paths represent all possible correct programs to solve the given problem. At each level, the programmer examines the alternative solutions and chooses the one that appears most suitable. However, if at any time the choice seems unwise, it is possible to backtrack one or more levels and select an alternative solution.

A tree illustrating the top-down approach is shown in Figure 54. It represents the hierarchical structure of a specific program for which five levels were needed. The top node is the main program, and the nodes at each successive level are the refined submodules that were introduced but undeveloped in the prior level. By the time the bottom level is reached, we have all the modules that comprise the final program.

The top-down approach is a programming technique that can be widely applied for good results. The technique does not necessarily guarantee the best solution, but it does provide a good structure for solving programming problems. The play of this chapter has been devoted to one example that illustrates precisely how the top-down method is used to write well-structured modular programs. The example also demonstrates that the method is, by and large, language independent.

Figure 54.   *Top-down structure for a specific program*

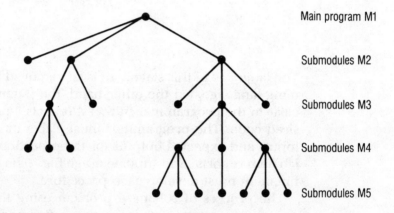

Main program M1

Submodules M2

Submodules M3

Submodules M4

Submodules M5

EXERCISES FOR PART III

Exercise 1 Programming Proverbs
List three ways in which Sam and Linda followed the proverb "Remember Your Reader."

Exercise 2 Programming Approaches
Write a short position paper comparing the "top-down" approach with the "systems analyst" approach of Chapter 2.

Exercise 3 The Input/Output Mapping
Develop an alternative to the condition-action list method for expressing how a program is to map input situations to output responses. Consider a decision table approach.

Exercise 4 Program Levels
Draw a complete tree in the form of Figure 54 to illustrate the levels of the Kriegspiel program.

Exercise 5 Program Modification
Modify the Kriegspiel program to accept moves in a completely free format, that is, without requiring column placement of the two squares.

Exercise 6 Program Critique
List five parts of the Kriegspiel program that, from a quality point of view, can be improved.

Exercise 7 Speeding Up a Program
Discuss five different ways for speeding up the Kriegspiel program. If you had to pick one way, which would cause the greatest speedup?

Exercise 8 Program Development
Write both an informal and formal statement of the module "EVALUATEMOVE" for the Kriegspiel program.

Exercise 9 Program Development
Following the same specification and top-down development strategy as Linda's, present a complete program to solve the following problem:

Input   A sequence of characters representing the text of a letter. The text contains only alphabetic English words, blanks, commas, periods, and the special word "PP" denoting the beginning of a paragraph.

Output

1. *The number of words in the text.*

2. *The text given as input, printed according to the following format:*

   a. The first line of each paragraph is to be indented five spaces and successive lines are to be left- justified.

   b. One blank is to separate each word from the previous word, comma, or period.

   c. A word cannot be broken across lines.

CHAPTER

8 *SOME PARTING COMMENTS*

I would like to include in this final chapter a variety of thoughts on the notion of software quality. These thoughts have been partially expressed in previous chapters. They are neither new nor rigorously supported, but they do sum up a number of important issues.

Programmers are faced with numerous difficult problems. One point often confused is the difference between problem solving and programming. *Problem solving* (see Lewis, 1980) can be viewed as the act of developing an algorithm to solve a given problem, "programming" as the act of transforming an algorithm into the linguistic concepts of a given programming language. In its conception, this book is primarily about programming, not problem solving. The techniques discussed in it will not necessarily help the programmer find a more efficient method of sorting, a faster method for computing Fourier Transforms, or a better heuristic for a chess-playing program.

The programmer's task is usually an intricate combination of both problem solving and programming. The issues in problem solving are vital to writing effective computer programs. Yet it is now well-recognized that the "programming" of a given algorithm is far from trivial, and that the programmer should use all the available techniques of programming to ensure that his devised algorithm is clear. While good programming techniques will offer strong guidelines for the development of a good solution to a problem, we must admit that "programming," as conceived here, is only part of the programmer's task.

As mentioned earlier, the use of program flowcharts has been avoided in this text. As a method of program design, program flowcharts have been highly overvalued. The top-down approach to programming suppresses the use of these flowcharts in favor of highlighting a functional or procedural approach to program design. The case against program flowcharts is similar to the case against the goto. The lines and arrows can easily lead the user into a highly sequential mode of thinking. Furthermore, there is a tendency to think that once a program flowchart has been designed, the programming process is just about complete. Unfortunately, this is seldom the case. The programmer would be well-advised to try another approach whenever he or she thinks a program flowchart is needed.

Consider the Kriegspiel program of Chapter 5. In this program no complete module requires a listing of more than two pages of text, and most modules fit on a single page. This characteristic results from human engineering. We all know how difficult it can be to follow a long program. In any lengthy program, we usually try to abstract a logical portion of it that will give us an indication of its overall computation. Every programmer should recognize this fact and write each program so that each logical unit is clearly isolated on a page or two. Furthermore, as mentioned above, each unit should be definable in terms of simple input/output coordinates, avoiding the use of global variables, for these can easily destroy the real modularity of logical units.

As regards Pascal, there are three features to which we take strong objection. First is its inability to declare and initialize constant structures. In the Kriegspiel program presented earlier, we had problems of this sort. Notice the lengthy and uninspiring code to initialize the legal next move mappings. How nice to have had even a simple data statement as in Fortran.

Second, Pascal's use of scalars is limited, since user-defined (enumerated) scalar names cannot be input or output from a program. While it is nice to say a type includes RED, WHITE, and BLUE, you must input them in some other form, normally an integer, and internally convert these values into colors.

Third, the absence of a "break" character makes it very difficult to interpret long names. How nice it would be to use names like X_COORDINATE, NEXT_SQ, NUM_VALUES_READ. Trying to undo these long names when written without a break character is a time-consuming and unrewarding task. We strongly urge that future versions of Pascal allow the longer names to be punctuated by an appropriate break character.

There are many other issues that need to be investigated. Among these are the need for better training, the establishment of problem definition techniques, the development of a more manageable successor to Pascal, and the promotion of human factors. The final issue is the critical need to upgrade the entire programming effort.

With all of the interest in programming, progress is certainly on its way. We must discipline ourselves to this interest but only adopt what is really progressive. Perhaps the best motivation is to recall how much hard work went into the last program you wrote and also that the program you write today may be the program you will maintain next year.

A *SUMMARY OF PROGRAM STANDARDS*

❧

GENERAL REQUIREMENTS

[GEN-1]   Someone should be appointed to maintain and enforce the standards.

[GEN-2]   All full programs shall include comments like:

```
{ -- ** Program Title:     Brief title
  -- ** Written By:        Name of author(s)
  -- ** Date Written:      Date
  --
  -- ** Program Summary:   Brief program summary
     ...
  -- ** Input and Output Files:
  --      file-name:       Brief description of use }
     ...
```

[GEN-3]   For each application there should be an adopted set of standard user-defined names and abbreviations.

[GEN-4]   Comments that occupy a full line must begin with -- and be written in lowercase.

[GEN-5]   No program unit should exceed two pages in length.

[GEN-6]   Each procedure or function should begin on a new page, (or for short procedures and functions) with a break of at least four blank lines.

[GEN-7]   Each line should have fewer than 72 characters.

[GEN-8]   Each statement must begin on a separate line.

DECLARATIONS

[DCL-1]   All scalars (numbers and characters) that remain constant throughout a program must be specified in a constant declaration.

[DCL-2]   All types must be named.

[DCL-3]   No function may change the values of its arguments.

[DCL-4]   The parameters of a procedure should be declared with comments describing the logical role of each parameter.

[DCL-5]   Each field in a record should be declared separately.

[DCL-6]   The keywords CONST, TYPE, and VAR should occupy a line by themselves.

[DCL-7]   The bodies of constant, type, and variable declarations must be indented from the beginning of the corresponding header keywords.

CONTROL STRUCTURES

[CONTROL-1]   Goto's are not allowed.

[CONTROL-2]   Nesting of any combination of if, for, while, with, case, and repeat statements must be no more than four levels deep. A generalized case statement simulating a "select-first" is counted as one level.

[CONTROL-3]   Null statements must include a comment line, for example, {do nothing}

[CONTROL-4]   Compound while and for statements are displayed similarly to repeat statements.

[CONTROL-5]   If statements are displayed in a comblike fashion rather than a nested fashion.

[CONTROL-6]   The bodies of begin-end, for, repeat, while, with, and case statements, as well as the bodies of record-end structures, must be indented from their corresponding header and closing keywords.

SPACING

[SPACE-1]   A uniform indentation of three spaces is to be used.

[SPACE-2]   At least one space is put before and after "=", ":=", and each relational operator.

[SPACE-3]   At least one space is put after each ":" in declarations.

[SPACE-4]   At least one space is put after each ":" and ";" in parameter lists.

[SPACE-5]   A space should be used as in normal English usage.

B FINAL PROGRAM FOR KRIEGSPIEL CHECKERS

❧

```
-- ** Written By:   Samuel Williams and Janet Raymond
-- ** Date Written: July, 1985
-- ** Written for:  Software Development Group
-- ** Version:      1 (Version 2 will include a board display
--                     for each of the players.)
--
-- ** Program Intent:
--
-- This program acts as the referee for the game of Kriegspiel
-- Checkers. The input to this program consists of a series of
-- moves taken from two interactive terminals. The output is a
-- sequence of messages informing the players of the current
-- game status. A copy of each player's pieces is shown on
-- a standard checkerboard maintained on the screen.
--
--                    BLACK
--
--           1     2     3     4
--        5     6     7     8
--           9    10    11    12
--       13    14    15    16
--          17    18    19    20
--       21    22    23    24
--          25    26    27    28
--       29    30    31    32
--
--                    RED
--
--
--
```

```
-- ** Rules of Kriegspiel:
--
-- (a)  Black moves first.
-- (b)  Players take alternate moves: black, then white, etc.
-- (c)  A player moves forward only, along diagonal paths.
-- (d)  A simple move is one square forward to an vacant square.
-- (e)  A jump move requires an opponent's piece on the next
--      forward square and a vacant square beyond.
-- (f)  If one or more jumps are possible for a player, then the move
--      must be a jump move. If a jump can be continued to jump
--      another piece, the jump must be continued.
-- (g)  When the move is a jump, the opponent's piece is
--      removed from the board. The piece is said to be "captured."
-- (h)  The game is won when a player either
--      (1) captures all of the opponent's pieces,
--      (2) places a piece on the opponent's back row (the king row), or
--      (3) blocks all of the opponent's pieces so that none can move.
--
-- ** Major Data Structures:
--
-- BOARD gives the status of each of the 32 squares, i.e., whether the
-- square is occupied by a red piece, a black piece, or  neither (vacant).
--
-- LEFTADJSQ, RIGHTADJSQ, LEFTJUMPSQ, and RIGHTJUMPSQ
-- indicate the possible paths that a black (or red) piece
-- can take from a given square. There are 32 entries,
-- corresponding to the 32 squares on the board. Each entry
-- is a square number or zero (meaning no legal path).
-- For instance
--
--    LEFTADJSQ  [BLACK, 17]  =  21
--    RIGHTADJSQ [BLACK, 17]  =  22
--    LEFTJUMPSQ [BLACK, 17]  =  0
--    RIGHTJUMPSQ[BLACK, 17]  =  26
--
-- ** Input and Output Files:
--
-- BLACKSTERMINAL   I/O device for player with black pieces.
-- REDSTERMINAL     I/O device for player with red pieces. }
```

```
program KRIEGSPIEL (BLACKSTERMINAL, REDSTERMINAL);
    const
        NULLSQ = 0;
        NUMSQS = 32;
        MAXLINESIZE = 72;
        BLANK = ' ';

    type
        COLOR    = (BLACK, RED);
        SQSTATUS = (BLACKPIECE, REDPIECE, VACANT);

        INPUTSTATUS =
            (ILLEGALSQ,    NOSEPARATOR, SQOUTOFRANGE,  MOVEOK,
             ILLEGALMOVE, JUMPEXISTS,  JUMP,          JUMPCONT);

        MSGNAME =
            (ILLEGALSQMSG,    NOSEPARATORMSG, SQOUTOFRANGEMSG,
             ILLEGALMOVEMSG, JUMPEXISTSMSG,   MOVEOKMSG,
             NEWMOVEMSG,     JUMPCONTMSG,     PIECETAKENMSG,
             BLACKINTROMSG,  REDINTROMSG,     WINNINGMSG, LOSINGMSG);

        SQVALUE     = 1..NUMSQS;
        DESTINATION = NULLSQ..NUMSQS;

        MOVEPAIR = record
                       SQ1: SQVALUE;
                       SQ2: SQVALUE
                   end;

        BOARDCONTENTS = array [1..NUMSQS] of SQSTATUS;
        ADJACENTSQS   = array [COLOR, 1..NUMSQS] of DESTINATION;
        INPUTBUFFER   = array [1..MAXLINESIZE] of CHAR;
    var
        BLACKSTERMINAL, REDSTERMINAL: TEXT;
        PLAYER, OPPONENT: COLOR;

        BOARD: BOARDCONTENTS;

        LEFTADJSQ, LEFTJUMPSQ,
        RIGHTADJSQ, RIGHTJUMPSQ: ADJACENTSQS;

        MOVE: MOVEPAIR;
        MOVESTATUS: INPUTSTATUS;

        CONTINUESQ: SQVALUE;
        GAMEOVER,
        JUMPAGAIN: BOOLEAN;
```

```pascal
procedure INITIALIZE (var BOARD: BOARDCONTENTS);
    const
        FIRSTBLACKSQ   = 1;
        LASTBLACKSQ    = 12;
        FIRSTVACANTSQ  = 13;
        LASTVACANTSQ   = 20;
        FIRSTREDSQ     = 21;
        LASTREDSQ      = 32;
    var
        SQ: SQVALUE;
begin
    for SQ := FIRSTBLACKSQ to LASTBLACKSQ do
        BOARD[SQ] := BLACKPIECE;

    for SQ := FIRSTVACANTSQ to LASTVACANTSQ do
        BOARD[SQ] := VACANT;

    for SQ := FIRSTREDSQ to LASTREDSQ do
        BOARD[SQ] := REDPIECE
end;
```

```
procedure SETUPBLACK ({setting} var LEFTADJSQ, LEFTJUMPSQ,
                          RIGHTADJSQ, RIGHTJUMPSQ: ADJACENTSQS);

{ -- This procedure establishes the legal adjacent squares for BLACK.
  -- "Left and "Right" are as viewed from the bottom of the board. }
var
   SQ: SQVALUE;
begin
   { -- left adjacent paths }
   for SQ := 1 to 32 do
      if SQ in [1, 2, 3, 4,  9, 10, 11, 12, 17, 18, 19, 20,
                25, 26, 27, 28] then
         LEFTADJSQ[BLACK, SQ] := SQ + 4
      else if SQ in [6, 7, 8,  14, 15, 16,  22, 23, 24] then
         LEFTADJSQ[BLACK, SQ] := SQ + 3
      else
         LEFTADJSQ[BLACK, SQ] := NULLSQ;

   { -- left jump paths }
   for SQ := 1 to 32 do
      if SQ in [2, 3, 4,  6, 7, 8, 10, 11, 12, 14, 15, 16, 18, 19, 20,
                22, 23, 24] then
         LEFTJUMPSQ[BLACK, SQ] := SQ + 7
      else
         LEFTJUMPSQ[BLACK, SQ] := NULLSQ;

   { -- right adjacent paths }
   for SQ := 1 to 32 do
      if SQ in [1, 2, 3,  9, 10, 11, 17, 18, 19, 25, 26, 27] then
         RIGHTADJSQ[BLACK, SQ] := SQ + 5
      else if SQ in [5, 6, 7, 8, 13, 14, 15, 16, 21, 22, 23, 24] then
         RIGHTADJSQ[BLACK, SQ] := SQ + 4
      else
         RIGHTADJSQ[BLACK, SQ] := NULLSQ;

   { -- right jump paths }
   for SQ := 1 to 32 do
      if SQ in [1, 2, 3, 5, 6, 7, 9, 10, 11, 13, 14, 15, 17, 18, 19,
                21, 22, 23] then
         RIGHTJUMPSQ[BLACK, SQ] := SQ + 9
      else
         RIGHTJUMPSQ[BLACK, SQ] := NULLSQ
end;
```

```
procedure SETUPRED ({setting} var LEFTADJSQ, LEFTJUMPSQ,
                          RIGHTADJSQ, RIGHTJUMPSQ: ADJACENTSQ);

{ -- This procedure establishes the legal adjacent squares for RED. }
   var
      SQ: SQVALUE;
begin
   { -- left adjacent paths }
   for SQ := 1 to 32 do
      if SQ in [6, 7, 8, 14, 15, 16, 22, 23, 24, 30, 31, 32] then
         LEFTADJSQ[RED, SQ] := SQ - 5
      else if SQ in [9, 10, 11, 12, 17, 18, 19, 20,
                     25, 26, 27, 28] then
         LEFTADJSQ[RED, SQ] := SQ - 4
      else
         LEFTADJSQ[RED, SQ] := NULLSQ;

   { -- left jump paths }
   for SQ := 1 to 32 do
      if SQ in [10, 11, 12, 14, 15, 16, 18, 19, 20,
                22, 23, 24, 26, 27, 28, 30, 31, 32] then
         LEFTJUMPSQ[RED, SQ] := SQ - 9
      else
         LEFTJUMPSQ[RED, SQ] := NULLSQ;

   { -- right adjacent paths }
   for SQ := 1 to 32 do
      if SQ in [5, 6, 7, 8,  13, 14, 15, 16,
                21, 22, 23, 24, 29, 30, 31, 32] then
         RIGHTADJSQ[RED, SQ] := SQ - 4
      else if SQ in [9, 10, 11,  17, 18, 19, 25, 26, 27] then
         RIGHTADJSQ[RED, SQ] := SQ - 3
      else
         RIGHTADJSQ[RED, SQ] := NULLSQ;

   [ -- right jump paths }
   for SQ := 1 to 32 do
      if SQ in [9, 10, 11, 13, 14, 15, 17, 18, 19,
                21, 22, 23, 25, 26, 27, 29, 30, 31] then
         RIGHTJUMPSQ[RED, SQ] := SQ - 7
      else
         RIGHTJUMPSQ[RED, SQ] := NULLSQ
end;
```

```
procedure SENDMSG ({to}    PLAYER: COLOR;
                   {using} MSGID:  MSGNAME);

{ -- Note: The assignment of devices for I/O is a nonstandard
  -- implementation-dependent feature. }

    var
       DEVICE: TEXT;

begin
    if PLAYER = BLACK then
       ASSIGN (DEVICE, BLACKSTERMINAL)
    else
       ASSIGN (DEVICE, REDSTERMINAL);
    WRITELN (DEVICE);

    case MSGID of
       BLACKINTROMSG:
          begin
             WRITELN (DEVICE, 'WELCOME TO KRIEGSPIEL CHECKERS.');
             WRITELN (DEVICE, 'MOVES ARE GIVEN AS TWO SQUARE NUMBERS ',
                              'FOR INSTANCE, 9 14');
          end;

       REDINTROMSG:
          begin
             WRITELN (DEVICE, 'WELCOME TO KRIEGSPIEL CHECKERS.');
             WRITELN (DEVICE, 'MOVES ARE GIVEN AS TWO SQUARE NUMBERS ',
                              'FOR INSTANCE, 21 17');
             WRITELN (DEVICE, 'YOUR OPPONENT WILL MAKE THE FIRST MOVE.')
          end;

       NEWMOVEMSG:
          WRITE (DEVICE, 'IT IS YOUR TURN TO MOVE: ');

       MOVEOKMSG:
          WRITELN (DEVICE, 'OK, YOUR OPPONENT HAS BEEN ASKED TO MOVE.');

       JUMPCONTMSG:
          begin
             WRITELN (DEVICE, 'YOUR JUMP MUST BE CONTINUED.');
             WRITE   (DEVICE, 'ENTER JUMP SQUARE ONLY: ');
          end;

       PIECETAKENMSG:
          WRITELN (DEVICE, 'PIECE CAPTURED. ');
```

```
            ILLEGALMOVEMSG:
              WRITE (DEVICE, 'TRY AGAIN: ');

            JUMPEXISTSMSG:
              begin
                WRITELN (DEVICE, 'A JUMP IS AVAILABLE AND YOU MUST TAKE IT.'
                WRITE   (DEVICE, 'TRY AGAIN: ')
              end;

            NOSEPARATORMSG:
              begin
                WRITELN (DEVICE, 'NO SPACE OR COMMA BETWEEN SQUARES.');
                WRITE   (DEVICE, 'TRY AGAIN: ')
              end;

            ILLEGALSQMSG:
              begin
                WRITELN (DEVICE, 'NON-NUMERIC CHARACTERS IN SQUARE NUMBER.');
                WRITE   (DEVICE, 'TRY AGAIN: ')
              end;

            SQOUTOFRANGEMSG:
              begin
                WRITELN (DEVICE, 'SQUARE NUMBER OUT OF RANGE 1 TO 32.');
                WRITE   (DEVICE, 'TRY AGAIN: ')
              end;
            LOSINGMSG:
              WRITELN (DEVICE, 'SORRY. . .YOUR OPPONENT HAS WON THE GAME!!!');

            WINNINGMSG:
              WRITELN (DEVICE, 'CONGRATULATIONS. . .YOU HAVE WON THE GAME!!!');
        end
    end;

  function DIGITVAL (C: CHAR): {returns} INTEGER;
  begin
    DIGITVAL := ORD(C) - ORD('0')
  end;
```

```
procedure SWAP (var PLAYER,  OPPONENT: COLOR);

   var
      OLDPLAYER: COLOR;

begin
   OLDPLAYER := PLAYER;
   PLAYER    := OPPONENT;
   OPPONENT  := OLDPLAYER
end;

procedure GETLINE ({from}      PLAYER: COLOR;
                   {into}  var BUFFER: INPUTBUFFER );

{ -- This procedure obtains a line of input from a player.
  -- The input line is right-padded with blanks up to
  -- MAXLINESIZE characters. }

   var
      CHARPOS: INTEGER;

begin
   for CHARPOS := 1 to MAXLINESIZE do
      BUFFER[CHARPOS] := BLANK;
   CHARPOS := 1;

   case PLAYER of
      BLACK: begin
                while not EOLN(BLACKSTERMINAL)
                and (CHARPOS <= MAXLINESIZE) do begin
                   READ (BLACKSTERMINAL, BUFFER[CHARPOS]);
                   CHARPOS := CHARPOS + 1
                end;
                READLN (BLACKSTERMINAL)
             end;

      RED:  begin
                while not EOLN(REDSTERMINAL)
                and (CHARPOS <= MAXLINESIZE) do begin
                   READ (REDSTERMINAL, BUFFER[CHARPOS]);
                   CHARPOS := CHARPOS + 1
                end;
                READLN (REDSTERMINAL)
             end
   end
end;
```

```pascal
procedure GETONESQ ({from}   PLAYER: COLOR;
                    {giving} var LINESTATUS: INPUTSTA
                             var SQ: SQVALUE);

    var
       NUM: INTEGER;
       INPUTLINE: INPUTBUFFER;
       CHAR1, CHAR2: CHAR;

begin
    GETLINE (PLAYER, INPUTLINE);
    LINESTATUS := MOVEOK;
    CHAR1 := INPUTLINE[1];
    CHAR2 := INPUTLINE[2];

    if (CHAR1 in ['0'..'9']) and not (CHAR2 in ['0'..'9']) then
        NUM := DIGITVAL(CHAR1)
    else if (CHAR1 in ['0'..'9']) and (CHAR2 in ['0'..'9']) then
        NUM := 10 * DIGITVAL(CHAR1) + DIGITVAL(CHAR2)
    else
        LINESTATUS := ILLEGALSQ;

    if (LINESTATUS = MOVEOK) then begin
        if NUM in [1..32] then
            SQ := NUM
        else
            LINESTATUS := SQOUTOFRANGE
    end
end;
```

```
procedure GETTWOSQS ({from} PLAYER: COLOR;
                     {giving} var LINESTATUS: INPUTSTATUS;
                              var SQ1: SQVALUE;
                              var SQ2: SQVALUE);

  const
    COMMA = ',';
  var
    INPUTLINE: INPUTBUFFER;
    CHAR1, CHAR2, CHAR3, CHAR4, CHAR5: CHAR;
    NUM1, NUM2: INTEGER;

begin
  GETLINE (PLAYER, INPUTLINE);
  LINESTATUS := MOVEOK;
  CHAR1 := INPUTLINE[1];
  CHAR2 := INPUTLINE[2];
  CHAR3 := INPUTLINE[3];
  CHAR4 := INPUTLINE[4];
  CHAR5 := INPUTLINE[5];

  if (CHAR1 in ['0'..'9']) and (CHAR2 in [BLANK, COMMA]) then
     begin
        NUM1 := DIGITVAL(CHAR1);
        if (CHAR3 in ['0'..'9'])
        and not (CHAR4 in ['0'..'9']) then
           NUM2 := DIGITVAL(CHAR3)
        else if (CHAR3 in ['0'..'9'])
        and (CHAR4 in ['0'..'9']) then
           NUM2 := 10 * DIGITVAL(CHAR3) + DIGITVAL(CHAR4)
        else
           LINESTATUS := ILLEGALSQ
     end
  else if (CHAR1 in ['0'..'9']) and (CHAR2 in ['0'..'9'])
     and (CHAR3 in [BLANK, COMMA]) then
     begin
        NUM1 := 10 * DIGITVAL(CHAR1) + DIGITVAL(CHAR2);
        if (CHAR4 in ['0'..'9'])
        and not (CHAR5 in ['0'..'9']) then
           NUM2 := DIGITVAL(CHAR4)
        else if (CHAR4 in ['0'..'9']) and CHAR5 in ['0'..'9']) then
           NUM2 := 10 * DIGITVAL(CHAR4) + DIGITVAL(CHAR5)
        else
           LINESTATUS := ILLEGALSQ
     end
  else if not (CHAR1 in ['0'..'9']) then
     LINESTATUS := ILLEGALSQ
```

```
      else
         LINESTATUS := NOSEPARATOR;
      if LINESTATUS = MOVEOK then begin
         if (NUM1 in [1..32]) and (NUM2 in [1..32]) then
            begin
               SQ1 := NUM1;
               SQ2 := NUM2
            end
         else
            LINESTATUS := SQOUTOFRANGE
      end
   end;
```

```
procedure GETONESQMOVE ({from} PLAYER:      COLOR;
                        {using} CONTINUESQ: SQVALUE;
                        {giving} var MOVE:  MOVEPAIR);

{ -- This procedure prompts for a jump continuation square
  -- until a valid square number is entered. }

    var
       LINESTATUS: INPUTSTATUS;
       SQFOUND:    BOOLEAN;
       NEWSQ:      SQVALUE;

begin
   SQFOUND := FALSE;
   repeat
      GETONESQ (PLAYER, LINESTATUS, NEWSQ);

      case LINESTATUS of
         ILLEGALSQ:    SENDMSG (PLAYER, ILLEGALSQMSG);
         SQOUTOFRANGE: SENDMSG (PLAYER, SQOUTOFRANGEMSG);
         MOVEOK:       SQFOUND := TRUE
         end
   until SQFOUND;

   MOVE.SQ1 := CONTINUESQ;
   MOVE.SQ2 := NEWSQ
end;
```

```
procedure GETTWOSQMOVE ({from} PLAYER: COLOR;
                        {giving} var MOVE: MOVEPAIR);

{ -- This procedure prompts for the two squares in a normal
  -- (nonjump continuation) move. Prompting continues until
  -- two valid square numbers are entered. }

    var
       LINESTATUS: INPUTSTATUS;
       SQSFOUND:   BOOLEAN;
       NEWSQ1, NEWSQ2: SQVALUE;

begin
    SQSFOUND := FALSE;
    repeat
      GETTWOSQS (PLAYER, LINESTATUS, NEWSQ1, NEWSQ2);

      case LINESTATUS of
         ILLEGALSQ:    SENDMSG (PLAYER, ILLEGALSQMSG);
         SQOUTOFRANGE: SENDMSG (PLAYER, SQOUTOFRANGEMSG);
         NOSEPARATOR:  SENDMSG (PLAYER, NOSEPARATORMSG);
         MOVEOK:       SQSFOUND := TRUE
      end
    until SQSFOUND;

    MOVE.SQ1 := NEWSQ1;
    MOVE.SQ2 := NEWSQ2
end;
```

```
function JUMPPATHFREE ({on}   var BOARD: BOARDCONTENTS;
                       {for}  PLAYER: COLOR;
                       {from} SQ: SQVALUE): BOOLEAN;


   var
      OPPONENTSPIECE: BLACKPIECE..REDPIECE;
      PATHFOUND:      BOOLEAN;

begin
   if PLAYER = BLACK then
      OPPONENTSPIECE := REDPIECE
   else
      OPPONENTSPIECE := BLACKPIECE;
   PATHFOUND := FALSE;

   if LEFTJUMPSQ[PLAYER, SQ] <> NULLSQ then
      if (BOARD[ LEFTJUMPSQ[PLAYER, SQ] ] = VACANT)
      and (BOARD[ LEFTADJSQ[PLAYER, SQ] ] = OPPONENTSPIECE) then
         PATHFOUND := TRUE;

   if RIGHTJUMPSQ[PLAYER, SQ] <> NULLSQ then
      if (BOARD[ RIGHTJUMPSQ[PLAYER, SQ] ] = VACANT)
      and (BOARD[ RIGHTADJSQ[PLAYER, SQ] ] = OPPONENTSPIECE) then
         PATHFOUND := TRUE;

   JUMPPATHFREE := PATHFOUND
end;
```

```
function PATHFREE ({on}    var BOARD: BOARDCONTENTS;
                   {for}   PLAYER: COLOR;
                   {from}  SQ: SQVALUE):  BOOLEAN;

    var
        PATHFOUND: BOOLEAN;
        PLAYERSPIECE: SQSTATUS;
        LEFTSQ, RIGHTSQ: DESTINATION;

begin
    if PLAYER = BLACK then
        PLAYERSPIECE := BLACKPIECE
    else
        PLAYERSPIECE := REDPIECE;
    PATHFOUND := FALSE;

    LEFTSQ  := LEFTADJSQ[PLAYER, SQ];
    RIGHTSQ := RIGHTADJSQ[PLAYER, SQ];
    if BOARD[SQ] = PLAYERSPIECE then begin
        if LEFTSQ <> NULLSQ then
            if BOARD[LEFTSQ] = VACANT then
                PATHFOUND :  TRUE;
        if RIGHTSQ <> NULLSQ then
            if BOARD[RIGHTSQ] = VACANT then
                PATHFOUND := TRUE
    end;

    if PATHFOUND then
        PATHFREE := PATHFOUND
    else
        PATHFREE := JUMPPATHFREE (BOARD, PLAYER, SQ)
end;
```

```
function JUMPAVAILABLE ({on} var BOARD: BOARDCONTENTS;
                        {for} PLAYER: COLOR):  BOOLEAN;

   var
      SQNUM:      0..NUMSQS;
      JUMPFOUND: BOOLEAN;

begin
   SQNUM := 0;
   JUMPFOUND := FALSE;

   repeat
      SQNUM := SQNUM + 1;
      case PLAYER of
         BLACK:
            if BOARD[SQNUM] = BLACKPIECE then
               JUMPFOUND := JUMPPATHFREE (BOARD, PLAYER, SQNUM);
         RED:
            if BOARD[SQNUM] = REDPIECE then
               JUMPFOUND := JUMPPATHFREE (BOARD, PLAYER, SQNUM)
      end
   until JUMPFOUND or (SQNUM = NUMSQS);

   JUMPAVAILABLE := JUMPFOUND
end;
```

```pascal
function NOMOVESLEFT ({for} PLAYER: COLOR;
                      {on} var BOARD: BOARDCONTENTS):  BOOLEAN;

{ -- Tests if all pieces are blocked. }

    var
        SQNUM:     0..NUMSQS;
        MOVEFOUND: BOOLEAN;

begin
    SQNUM := 0;
    MOVEFOUND := FALSE;

    repeat
        SQNUM := SQNUM + 1;
        case PLAYER of
            BLACK:
                if BOARD[SQNUM] = BLACKPIECE then
                    MOVEFOUND := PATHFREE (BOARD, PLAYER, SQNUM);
            RED:
                if BOARD[SQNUM] = REDPIECE then
                    MOVEFOUND := PATHFREE (BOARD, PLAYER, SQNUM)
        end
    until MOVEFOUND or (SQNUM = NUMSQS);

    NOMOVESLEFT := not MOVEFOUND
end;
```

```
function GAMEWON ({for} PLAYER: COLOR;
                  {on} var BOARD: BOARDCONTENTS):  BOOLEAN;

{ -- Checks status of the king row and total blocking. }

begin
  case PLAYER of
    BLACK:
        if (BLACKPIECE in [BOARD[29], BOARD[30], BOARD[31], BOARD[32]])
        or (NOMOVESLEFT(RED, BOARD)) then
          GAMEWON := TRUE
        else
          GAMEWON := FALSE;


    RED:
        if (REDPIECE in [BOARD[1], BOARD[2], BOARD[3], BOARD[4]])
        or (NOMOVESLEFT (BLACK, BOARD)) then
          GAMEWON := TRUE
        else
          GAMEWON := FALSE
  end
end;




procedure UPDATEBOARD ({for}   PLAYER: COLOR;
                       {using} MOVE: MOVEPAIR;
                       {updating}  var BOARD: BOARDCONTENTS);
  var
    SQ1, SQ2: SQVALUE;

begin
  SQ1 := MOVE.SQ1;
  SQ2 := MOVE.SQ2;

  BOARD[SQ2] := BOARD[SQ1];
  BOARD[SQ1] := VACANT;

  if LEFTJUMPSQ[PLAYER, SQ1] = SQ2 then
     BOARD[ LEFTADJSQ[PLAYER, SQ1] ] := VACANT
  else if RIGHTJUMPSQ[PLAYER, SQ1] = SQ2 then
     BOARD[ RIGHTADJSQ[PLAYER, SQ1] ] := VACANT
end;
```

```
procedure EVALUATEMOVE ({using} PLAYER: COLOR; MOVE: MOVEPAIR;
                                 BOARD: BOARDCONTENTS;
                        {giving} var MOVESTATUS: INPUTSTATUS);

   var
      SQ1, SQ2:      SQVALUE;
      PLAYERSPIECE:  SQSTATUS;
      OPPONENTSPIECE: SQSTATUS;
      ERROR:         BOOLEAN;

begin
   if PLAYER = BLACK then
      begin
         PLAYERSPIECE   := BLACKPIECE;
         OPPONENTSPIECE := REDPIECE
      end
   else
      begin
         PLAYERSPIECE   := REDPIECE;
         OPPONENTSPIECE := BLACKPIECE
      end;
   SQ1 := MOVE.SQ1;
   SQ2 := MOVE.SQ2;

   if (BOARD[SQ1] = PLAYERSPIECE) and (BOARD[SQ2] = VACANT) then
      case JUMPAVAILABLE (BOARD, PLAYER) of
         FALSE: if (LEFTADJSQ[PLAYER, SQ1] = SQ2)
                or (RIGHTADJSQ[PLAYER, SQ1] = SQ2) then
                   MOVESTATUS := MOVEOK
                else
                   MOVESTATUS := ILLEGALMOVE;

         TRUE: begin
                  if (LEFTJUMPSQ[PLAYER, SQ1] = SQ2) then
                     if BOARD[LEFTADJSQ[PLAYER, SQ1]] = OPPONENTSPIECE then
                        MOVESTATUS := JUMP
                     else
                        MOVESTATUS := ILLEGALMOVE
                  else if (RIGHTJUMPSQ[PLAYER, SQ1] = SQ2) then
                     if BOARD[RIGHTADJSQ[PLAYER, SQ1]] = OPPONENTSPIECE ↑
                        MOVESTATUS := JUMP
                     else
                        MOVESTATUS := ILLEGALMOVE
                  else
                     MOVESTATUS := JUMPEXISTS;

                  if (MOVESTATUS = JUMP)
```

```
                    and JUMPPATHFREE(BOARD, PLAYER, SQ2) then
                        MOVESTATUS := JUMPCONT
                end { begin }
        end { case }
    else
        MOVESTATUS := ILLEGALMOVE
end;



begin
    INITIALIZE (BOARD);
    SETUPBLACK (LEFTADJSQ, LEFTJUMPSQ, RIGHTADJSQ, RIGHTJUMPSQ);
    SETUPRED   (LEFTADJSQ, LEFTJUMPSQ, RIGHTADJSQ, RIGHTJUMPSQ);
    PLAYER   := BLACK;
    OPPONENT := RED;
    SENDMSG (OPPONENT, REDINTROMSG);
    SENDMSG (PLAYER,   BLACKINTROMSG);
    SENDMSG (PLAYER,   NEWMOVEMSG);

    GAMEOVER  := FALSE;
    JUMPAGAIN := FALSE;
    repeat
        if JUMPAGAIN then
            GETONESQMOVE ({using} PLAYER, CONTINUESQ, {giving} MOVE)
        else
            GETTWOSQMOVE ({using} PLAYER, {giving} MOVE);

        EVALUATEMOVE ({using} PLAYER, MOVE, BOARD, {giving} MOVESTATUS);
        case MOVESTATUS of
            JUMPEXISTS: SENDMSG (PLAYER, JUMPEXISTSMSG);
            ILLEGALMOVE: if JUMPAGAIN then
                            SENDMSG (PLAYER, JUMPCONTMSG)
                         else
                            SENDMSG (PLAYER, ILLEGALMOVEMSG);
            MOVEOK,
            JUMP:       begin
                            UPDATEBOARD (PLAYER, MOVE, BOARD);
                                if MOVESTATUS = JUMP then
                                    SENDMSG (PLAYER, PIECETAKENMSG);
                                if GAMEWON (PLAYER, BOARD) then
                                    GAMEOVER := TRUE
                                else
```

```
                              begin
                                  SENDMSG (PLAYER, MOVEOKMSG);
                                  SENDMSG (OPPONENT, NEWMOVEMSG);
                                  SWAP (PLAYER,  OPPONENT);
                                  JUMPAGAIN := FALSE
                              end
                          end;
              JUMPCONT:   begin
                              UPDATEBOARD (PLAYER, MOVE, BOARD);
                              SENDMSG (PIECETAKENMSG);
                              SENDMSG (PLAYER, JUMPCONTMSG);
                              JUMPAGAIN := TRUE;
                              CONTINUESQ := MOVE.SQ2
                          end
          end
          until GAMEOVER;

          SENDMSG (PLAYER,   WINNINGMSG);
          SENDMSG (OPPONENT, LOSINGMSG)
      end.
```

BIBLIOGRAPHY

American National Standard Pascal Computer Programming
Language
ANSI-IEEE 770 X3.97-1983

The American Pascal Standard, with Annotations
Annotated by Henry Ledgard
Springer-Verlag, NY, 1984

ANS FORTRAN Standard, American National Standards
Committee, 1977

Russell M. Armstrong
Modular Programming in Cobol
John Wiley and Sons, NY, 1973

F. T. Baker
Chief Programmer Team Management of Production
Programming
IBM Systems Journal, Vol. 11, No. 1, 1972

William C. Cave
*A Method for Management Control of Software
Development*
CENTACS Software Report, No. 41
U.S. Army Electronics Division, Fort Monmouth, NJ, 1974

William C. Cave and Gilbert W. Maymon
Software Lifecycle Management
Macmillan Publishing Co., NY, 1984

Louis J. Chmura and Henry F. Ledgard
Cobol With Style
Hayden Publishing Company, Hasbrouck Heights, NJ, 1976

Richard Conway, David Gries, and E. Zimmerman
A Primer on Pascal
Winthrop Publishers, Inc., Cambridge, MA, 1976

Laura Cooper and Marilyn Smith
Standard Fortran: A Problem Solving Approach
Houghton Mifflin, Boston, MA, 1973

J. Daniel Cougar
"Evolution of Business System Analysis Techniques"
Computing Surveys, Vol. 5, No. 3, September, 1973

O. J. Dahl, E. W. Dijkstra, and C. A. R. Hoare
Structured Programming
Academic Press, NY, 1972

Edsgar W. Dijkstra
"Goto Statement Considered Harmful"
Communications of the ACM, Vol. 11, No. 3, March, 1968

Edsgar W. Dijkstra
"The Humble Programmer," 1972 Turing Award Lecture
Communications of the ACM, Vol. 15, No. 10, October, 1972

Richard Fairley
Software Engineering Concepts
McGraw-Hill, NY, 1985

H. H. Goldstine and J. von Neumann
"Planning and Coding for an Electronic Computing
Instrument—Part II, Vol. 1"
John von Neumann—Collected Works, Vol. 5, Pergamon
Press, NY, 1963

Kathleen Jensen and Niklaus Wirth
Pascal User Manual and Report
Springer-Verlag, NY, Third Edition, 1985

Brian Kernighan and William Plauger
The Elements of Programming Style
McGraw-Hill, NY, 1973

Charles B. Kreitzberg and Ben Shneiderman
The Elements of Fortran Style: Techniques for Effective Programming
Harcourt Brace Jovanovich, NY, 1972

Henry F. Ledgard
Programming Proverbs
Hayden Book Co., Hasbrouck Heights, NJ, 1975

Henry F. Ledgard
Programming Proverbs for Fortran Programmers
Hayden Book Co., Hasbrouck Heights, NJ, 1975

Henry Ledgard, Paul Nagin, and Jon Hueras
Pascal With Style
Hayden Book Co., Hasbrouck Heights, NJ 1979

Henry F. Ledgard and William Cave
"Cobol Under Control"
Communications of the ACM, November, 1976

Henry F. Ledgard and Michael Marcotty
"A Genealogy of Control Structures"
Communications of the ACM, November, 1975

Henry Ledgard and Andrew Singer
Pascal for the Macintosh
Addison Wesley, Reading, MA 1985

William E. Lewis
Problem Solving Principles for Programmers
Hayden Book Co., Hasbrouck Heights, NJ, 1980

Daniel D. McCracken
A Guide to Fortran IV Programming
John Wiley and Sons, NY, 1972

Harlan B. Mills
Mathematical Foundations for Structured Programs
Technical Report, FSC 72-6012
IBM Federal Systems Division, Gaithersburg, MD, 1972

Michael Spier
  The Typset-10 Codex Programmaticus
  Technical Report, Digital Equipment Corporation, 1974

Christopher Strachey
  "Systems Analysis and Programming"
  in *Readings from Scientific American*
  W. H. Freeman and Co., San Francisco, 1971

William Strunk, Jr., and E. B. White
  The Elements of Style
  Macmillan, NY, 1959

Donnie Van Tassel
  Program Style, Design, Efficiency, Debugging, and Testing
  Prentice-Hall, Englewood Cliffs, NJ, 1974

Gerald Weinberg
  The Psychology of Computer Programming
  Van Nostrand Reinhold, NY, 1971

Niklaus Wirth
  "Program Development by Stepwise Refinement"
  Communications of the ACM, Vol. 14, No. 4, April, 1971

E. Yourdon
  Techniques of Program Structure and Design
  Prentice-Hall, Englewood Cliffs, NJ, 1975

INDEX